ESSENTIALS

OF

BUSINESS BUDGETING

The WorkSmart Series

The Basics of Business Writing
Commonsense Time Management
Effective Employee Orientation
Essentials of Business Budgeting
Essentials of Total Quality Management
Fundamentals of Project Management
Goal Setting
Great Customer Service on the Telephone
How to Become a Skillful Interviewer
How to Recognize & Reward Employees
How to Speak and Listen Effectively
The Power of Self-Esteem
Productive Performance Appraisals
Resolving Conflicts on the Job
The Successful New Manager
Successful Team Building

ESSENTIALS
OF
BUSINESS
BUDGETING

Robert G. Finney

amacom

AMERICAN MANAGEMENT ASSOCIATION

THE WORKSMART SERIES

New York • Atlanta • Boston • Chicago • Kansas City • San Francisco • Washington, D.C.
Brussels • Toronto • Mexico City

This book is available at a special
discount when ordered in bulk quantities.
For information, contact Special Sales Department,
AMACOM, a division of American Management Association,
135 West 50th Street, New York, NY 10020.

*This publication is designed to provide accurate and authoritative
information in regard to the subject matter covered. It is sold with the
understanding that the publisher is not engaged in rendering legal,
accounting, or other professional service. If legal advice or other expert
assistance is required, the services of a competent professional person
should be sought.*

Library of Congress Cataloging-in-Publication Data

Finney, Robert G.
      Essentials of business budgeting / Robert G. Finney.
            p.   cm.—(The WorkSmart series)
      ISBN 0-8144-7836-0
      1. Budget in business. I. Title. II. Series.
HG4028.B8F559   1995
658.15'4—dc20   94-39941
                            CIP

Printing number

10 9 8 7 6 5 4 3 2 1

CONTENTS

PREFACE

They say that nothing is certain except death and taxes, but budgets in corporations come close. All sizable businesses prepare budgets, all managers are involved in them, and all employees are affected by them.

The budget is the financial plan of a company for the period of a year, predicting:

- The contents of the financial statements over that period
- The detailed financial results of all the company's organizational elements

Budgeting is important. If you want a management career, good budgets will help you succeed, while bad budgets can contribute to your downfall. Budgets done right can be a powerful tool in making you a good manager. Budgets done wrong can put you behind the eight ball in January and keep you there the entire year.

If you are not a manager, budgets are the things that enable you to get the "tools" and the help you need to do your job. If you need a junior associate or a new computer or whatever to get your work done, of course you have to convince your boss of the need and the payoff. However, if funds for those tools and help are not in the budget, chances are your boss will not be able to authorize them, even if convinced.

If you are responsible for a budget, keep in mind that a good budget:

- Explains what your organization can and cannot do
- Explains the support you need to meet your commitments

- Sets realistic goals for you and your people
- Helps you communicate with bosses, subordinates, and other organizations
- Shows your understanding of the company's financial realities
- Therefore, it helps you improve your operations and shows that you are ready for promotion

If you are not responsible for a budget, then you and your work are part of your boss's budget. If you can influence your boss to budget your work and needs properly, you have a leg up on doing a good job next year. On the other hand, a poor budget—one that does not correctly reflect your needs and what you can accomplish—will handicap you all year.

Therefore, it is worthwhile to understand budgets and learn how to do good budgeting, and helping you to do both is the purpose of this book.

We will focus on budgeting from the point of view of working managers and their key people, not that of accounting or the board of directors. We will cover what the budget is and what it is not, how budgets are put together and how they are used, and what to expect at budget time. Then we will concentrate on the work of budgeting: planning next year's work, generating the budget numbers, and getting the right budget approved.

In the process, you will see that budgeting is not mysterious. It takes work to do it right, but that work requires the same talents you needed to get the responsible job that you already have. And the best part is that the work you do to prepare good budgets is exactly the work that will show you are qualified to be a manager, and then help you manage better.

ESSENTIALS
OF
BUSINESS
BUDGETING

CHAPTER 1

WHAT A BUDGET IS

Budget in this book always means *annual* budget, covering a period of one year.

Let's start with a multiple-choice question. From the company viewpoint, the budget is:

a. A forecast of the year's financial results.
b. A plan of the year's work.
c. A communication of higher management's real objectives and priorities.
d. A principal control and measurement tool.
e. All of the above.

The right answer is e, "All of the above."

The budget predicts the contents of the company's financial statements—profit and loss, balance sheet, and statement of cash flows—over the year. It also predicts in detail the pertinent financial results, such as revenue and costs of all kinds, of all the organizational elements of the company.

Keep in mind that the budget is most fundamentally a *plan*. It shows the resources needed and how they will be used. Business resources are people, particular skills, machines, work space, and money.

The budget communicates the real objectives and priorities for the year, because work will not get done if resources are not budgeted for it. Say you are in an engineering design unit and have heard enthusiastic plans for a new widget. However, if you see no money in the budget for its design, you know it is not a priority project.

All elements of the company are measured on performance relative to budget, have to explain deviations from budget,

1

The term *unit* is used in this book to denote the first-level organizational element of a company, such as a sales branch office or a particular factory assembly operation. This book is aimed at unit managers and their key people.

and probably cannot get activities approved that are not in the budget. If you lead a group budgeted to contain four people, you may not be able to hire a fifth even if you badly need that person.

THE UNIT MANAGER'S VIEWPOINT

In most companies, every unit manager has to prepare a budget, which is summed and transformed with all other unit budgets successively into department, division, and company budgets. Smart managers get budget inputs from their key people. If they don't, smart key people get involved and volunteer inputs, because this is the only way they can get the resources to do the work expected of them.

Beyond understanding and providing context, unit managers and their key people need not be concerned with what the controller, the president, or the board of directors does with the budget. What unit managers and their key people need from their budget are:

- The work and outputs expected from the unit over the course of the year
- The approval of the resources needed to accomplish that work and those outputs
- The inputs, support, and assistance the unit will receive from other elements of the company

BUDGET FORMS

Most company budgets take the same form as the financial statements—profit and loss, balance sheet, and cash flow—that appear in the annual report, with two additions:

1. There is more detail and elaboration in particular areas where the president wants more visibility: revenue by product line, for example.
2. Budgets include quarterly and often monthly num-

No two companies' budget forms are exactly alike. We will not discuss variations in forms here, but only the kind of information required in budgets, with examples. You must learn your own company's forms from your boss or accounting.

bers, rather than just year-end predictions. Managements need to track results frequently, so timely action can be taken if needed.

The company budget thus probably predicts revenue, expense, profit, capital expenditure, and receipts and disbursements of cash expected each month during the year; and the value of balance sheet accounts like inventory, equipment, accounts payable, and long-term debt at the end of each month.

ACCOUNTING

While budgeting is not an accounting problem, the budget is ultimately expressed in accounting terms. Every manager will benefit from knowledge of accounting fundamentals, but that is beyond the scope of this book. For ready reference, accounting terms that unit managers will encounter in budgeting are defined in the Glossary, at the end of the book.

The unit manager's budget, the first building block of that company budget, typically requires three types of information:

1. Costs
2. Outputs
3. Supplemental information

By far the most information required is predicted *costs*. The manager may be asked for "effort" descriptions—man-hours of effort, numbers of items purchased, etc.—that the accountants convert into dollars, or the manager may be asked to supply dollar numbers. Depending on the unit's function, cost prediction may be required in considerable detail. An engineering unit, for example, is usually required to forecast costs by project, because management wants to track the cost and profitability of each project.

Whether the predicted *outputs* of the unit are required depends on its function. Examples of functions for which outputs are required in the budget are numbers of different items completed by an assembly unit, and numbers of orders of different products by a sales unit. Such outputs are "financially significant," meaning that they ultimately relate directly to revenue. On the other hand, the number of pages expected to be produced by a word processing unit—its primary output—has no direct relation to revenue, so its predicted outputs are probably not required on the budget form.

Supplemental information required varies widely, but includes information that helps explain the budget (e.g., the number of cold calls per period planned by a sales function as a basis for the orders prediction), helps evaluate the budget (e.g., results for the previous three years for comparison), and the like. The assumptions made in preparing the budget are also often required as supplemental information.

As an example of a budget form, the payroll unit budget form shown in Figure 1 is about as simple as budget forms get.

Total cost is the sum of total salaries, fringe benefits (medical insurance and the like), and total other indirect costs (as itemized). Labor costs are just salaries, readily identified and tracked by individual names. The number and type of "other indirect" cost lines is determined by management's decision concerning the desired visibility of different kinds of costs. Every budget has an "other" category for costs not itemized, because the budget must include total costs. Typically, outputs are not required in a payroll unit budget.

Most budget forms require more information than this simple example, and may run for pages and pages. A factory assembly function is an example of a unit whose budget form is more extensive. The assembly manager is asked for

Figure 1.   Simple payroll unit budget form.

199_ Payroll Unit Budget	J F M	A M J	J A S	O N D	TOTAL
Salaries ($)					
(Name)	| | | |	| | | |	| | | |	| | | |	|
(Name)	| | | |	| | | |	| | | |	| | | |	|
(Name)	| | | |	| | | |	| | | |	| | | |	|
⋮	| | | |	| | | |	| | | |	| | | |	|
(Planned New Hire)	| | | |	| | | |	| | | |	| | | |	|
Total	| | | |	| | | |	| | | |	| | | |	|
Fringe Benefits ($)	| | | |	| | | |	| | | |	| | | |	|
Other Indirect Costs ($)					
Travel & Living	| | | |	| | | |	| | | |	| | | |	|
Telephone Expense	| | | |	| | | |	| | | |	| | | |	|
Subscriptions	| | | |	| | | |	| | | |	| | | |	|
Training	| | | |	| | | |	| | | |	| | | |	|
Office Supplies	| | | |	| | | |	| | | |	| | | |	|
Outside Services	| | | |	| | | |	| | | |	| | | |	|
Other	| | | |	| | | |	| | | |	| | | |	|
Total	| | | |	| | | |	| | | |	| | | |	|
Total Cost ($)	| | | |	| | | |	| | | |	| | | |	|
Supplemental Information	| | | |	| | | |	| | | |	| | | |	|
New Hires	| | | |	| | | |	| | | |	| | | |	|
Computer Hours	| | | |	| | | |	| | | |	| | | |	|

number of assemblies by item (i.e., its outputs), direct labor man-hours by project or product, indirect labor, and more varieties of other indirect costs (all by month). Supplemental information probably includes such things as predicted direct and indirect head count, machine usage in hours, new hires, and layoffs. All of these items have to be predicted for each month of the year, or at least for each quarter.

BUDGETS ARE NEVER PERFECT OR EASY

Budgets can never be perfect predictions, because the future is inherently uncertain:

- The outside world seldom behaves the way you wish it would, and most of the surprises are going to be unpleasant.
- Company management may change priorities, processes, and procedures during the year. It may even reorganize in a way that removes some of your unit's inputs and support.
- For new things or new ways to do old things, cost predictions can seldom be perfect.

This uncertainty is also the main source of the pain and frustration that characterize most budgeting processes:

- Managers not only have to predict a year ahead when they are not sure what will happen next Tuesday, but often fifteen months ahead, because they are probably asked for their budgets in September of the previous year.
- Top management wants the best results achievable, but unit managers know that they will be measured on performance against budget. Self-protection requires that they budget conservatively. These contradictory motives frustrate everyone from the president to the unit managers and their people.
- There is more psychology than arithmetic in budgeting. Since the boss is also uncertain about the future, the budgeter must judge what the boss will accept, question, or arbitrarily cut. If the boss always cuts submitted budgets by 5 percent, the budgeter should obviously add 5% to the costs believed necessary. Most budgeting "games" are much more complex, and are played in every budgeting process.

WHY PLAN?

Now, since the budget is most fundamentally the plan for the year's activity, you ask, "With so much uncertainty involved, why plan at all?" The uncertainty makes planning *more* important, not less. For one thing, if you are certain what will happen, you don't have to plan, do you? More practically, a plan is a "stake in the ground" that lets you know if something has changed, the important changes to which you must react, and those you can ignore. The ever present uncertainty means that plans must contain latitude and "what ifs?"

For example, store managers never know how many customers will show up on a particular day next July, but they have to plan how many clerks to have available. What they do is assume a reasonable range of numbers of customers and plan enough clerks to accommodate that range with adequate service and reasonable cost. They also perhaps include a provision for obtaining part-time help to handle a higher peak. With no plan, the manager would not know whether to react to a sudden high peak of customers by hiring more full-time clerks. With the plan, the manager analyzes data over a period of time plus new outside factors—like a new factory opening nearby—before deciding whether the number of full-time clerks needs to be changed.

WHAT A BUDGET IS NOT

Let's present some conclusions in the form of another multiple choice question. Budgeting is:

a. An accounting activity, not a management activity.
b. The concern of only top management.
c. Everybody's favorite subject.
d. Not important, because so much guessing is involved.
e. None of the above.

You guessed it, the answer is again e, in this case, "None of the above."

Accounting does the budgeting process coordination, the arithmetic, the scorekeeping, and some of the evaluation. However, the budget is most fundamentally a *plan* for the company and all its organizational elements. Planning is the unavoidable responsibility of the people charged with producing the outputs and getting the work done—that is, managers and their key people.

All managers must be involved, because the budget is what defines what is expected of their organizational elements, and the resources, inputs, and support they will have to get their work done.

Budgeting is nobody's favorite subject, from the president down. It is painful and frustrating, and it may come back to haunt those who created it during the year.

It is important *because* so much guessing is involved—because of the uncertainty of the future. The budget is also important because it is potentially the company's most useful planning document:

> The budget states what the company plans to do during the year in concrete terms of people, dollars, equipment; and the results expected in concrete terms of orders, sales, profit, and cash flow.

CHAPTER 2

HOW BUDGETS ARE PREPARED AND USED

Why *annual* budgets? Because the investment and lending communities keep score based on annual periods. Since the budget is both the plan and the scorecard, it must also focus on the same annual periods.

Let's try true or false this time. Only one of the following four statements is false. Which one?

a. Higher management and the board of directors want a budget because they want a prediction of how much business the company can expect to do, how much that will cost, and what the nature of the costs will be.

b. They want this because the company represents an investment for which they are responsible. They naturally want to know how much profit and cash flow they can expect from that investment.

c. Higher management prepares the total company budget.

d. Higher management must decide what the company should do differently to increase profits and cash flow, and therefore when to change strategies and actions.

The false statement is c. Theoretically, higher management could prepare the budget, but this makes no sense. Multiple levels of managers have been appointed to direct and be responsible for all the activities required by the company to conduct its business. Both because of their greater knowledge of the particular activities and because of their responsibility for them, all managers are expected to contribute to the plans and predictions for next year.

9

THE COMPANY BUDGET

The company budget is really a collection of budgets that predicts its important financial results: orders, sales, profit and loss (P&L), capital expenditures, cash flow, and balance sheet. The logical flow of these budgets is shown in Figure 2.

All units contribute costs to the company budget, some forecast orders and revenue or sales, and some budget capital expenditures. *Capital expenditures* are costs for equipment, facilities, and the like, that are expected to be used for a number of years. They are budgeted and accounted for separately from most costs, which are charged to the P&L, or "expensed." Balance sheet and cash flow budgets are ordinarily done by accounting, and usually do not involve unit managers beyond their cost and revenue inputs.

The company budget is built as a consolidation of budgets that match its organization structure. For example, consider a midsize product company with a functional organization reporting to the president:

> *Company*
>
>> Marketing
>> Sales
>> Engineering
>> Manufacturing

Figure 2.   Flowchart of company budget.

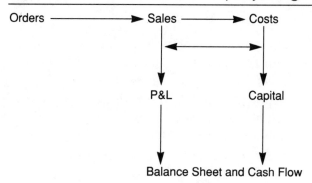

Finance
Human resources

Each of these major departments, of course, has an organizational structure within it; for simplicity, let's detail only the sales department (assuming only domestic sales and a geographical sales organization):

Sales

Eastern region sales
   New England branch
   Mid-Atlantic branch
   Southeastern branch
Central region sales
   Northern branch
   Southern branch
   Midwestern branch
Western region sales
   Southwestern branch
   Northwestern branch
   Rocky Mountain branch
Sales administration

Within the sales department, the first budgets generated are those for each of the branches ("units" in our nomenclature). All the Eastern region branch budgets are then consolidated into the Eastern region budget. The budgets of the three regions plus sales administration are then consolidated into the sales department budget. At the same time, the budgets of the other departments are built, level by level, in the same way. Finally, the company budget is the consolidation of all the department budgets.

The budget at each level is the *summation* of all the budgets at the next lower level, plus the costs and other budget items associated with the manager at that level. There is *summarization* of information at each level upward.

Company budgets are ultimately *expressed* in accounting and financial reporting terms ("financial" format), with the con-

A company's *fiscal year* is the twelve-month period for which financial results and statements are prepared and reported. For simplicity, we always assume that the fiscal year equals the calendar year.

cerns being revenue, expense, cash flow, and balance sheet items. The budgets used by higher management are in a format that presents the information desired to manage the business, typically a mixture of financial and activity formats. At the unit levels the budget concerns are man-hours, purchased items, transactions, and the like ("activity" format), which are ultimately expressed in dollars.

THE BUDGETING PROCESS

Preparation of the budget usually begins three to four months before the budget year begins. Thus, for a company whose fiscal year is the calendar year, budgeting probably starts in September.

Although each step contains complexity and hard work, the budgeting process can be described as these four simple steps:

1. Budget forms and instructions are distributed to all managers.
2. The budget forms are filled out and submitted.
3. The individual budgets are transformed into appropriate budgeting/accounting terms and consolidated into one overall company budget.
4. The budget is reviewed, modified as necessary, and approved.

Concerning the first step in the process, budget forms and the types of information required from unit managers were discussed in Chapter 1. At most companies, budget forms are pieces of paper, but some enlightened companies use diskettes formatted for personal computer use.

The instructions contain:

• The detailed schedule for the whole company budgeting process, culminating with presentation to the board of directors

- Assumptions and ground rules to be used throughout the company, division, or department
- General guidance, goals, and priorities for budget preparation
- Any changes in procedures or budget format from the previous year

The *completion and submission of budget forms* is the manager's activity of actually preparing the budget, the subject of the rest of this book.

The *transformation and consolidation* of the unit budgets are done by accounting:

- If unit managers submit budget numbers in terms of items and man-hours, these are translated into dollars.
- Allocated costs are added into the unit manager's budget.
- Burden rates are computed and applied when and as appropriate.
- As the process of consolidation moves up the organization, the activity format of the lower levels is transformed into the financial format used for the overall company.

At this point, it will be well worth your while to pause to read the accompanying box, which defines three important concepts for budgeters: allocated costs, cost burdens, and burden rates.

ALLOCATED COSTS, COST BURDENS, AND BURDEN RATES

Allocated costs are costs of one type that are assigned or charged to costs of other types. Every company has costs that are incurred and paid separately from its unit organizations but that are either used by the units (such as facility and telephone costs) or are general costs of doing business (such as management, legal, and accounting costs). Many such costs are typically charged, or *allocated,* to each unit of the particular business, based on mathematical formulas. For example, facility costs may be charged to a particular unit based on the square feet of space it occupies times the cost of the facility (rent, utilities, taxes) per square foot.

Cost burdens are the amount of costs added to a particular cost as the result of allocating another type of cost to it. Managements universally want to know the profitability of individual products they sell. For a manufacturing business, for example, they define *direct costs* as labor, materials, and other things that are directly related to producing the product. However, there are many costs that are necessary but only indirectly related to a particular product, everything from the manufacturing manager's salary to the costs of the human resources function. All such things are called *indirect costs*. Traditionally, direct costs are "burdened" with certain indirect costs to get a better measure of product profitability; that is, such indirect costs are a "cost burden" on the direct costs.

Burden rates are the rates at which these cost burdens are applied. If total indirect labor costs in the example manufacturing business are expected to be twice the total direct labor costs for the year, this defines a burden rate called "manufacturing labor overhead rate," equal to 200%. In this case, every dollar of direct labor involved in making a product results in $3 being charged to that particular product. That is, $1 + ($1 \times 200\%) = \$3$.

Different businesses use various burdens and burden rates. Common ones are manufacturing labor overhead rate, manufacturing material overhead rate, engineering overhead rate, and G&A rate. The latter is used to allocate *general and administrative expense (G&A)*, which is necessary expense that cannot even be indirectly related to the production of products or services, such as the costs of the president's office, board of directors, accounting, and human resources. G&A is often allocated to entire product or service lines based on their sales or cost of sales.

Transformation and consolidation are interleaved with the fourth step, *review, modification, and approval.* Together, they are a step-by-step, repetitive progression up the levels of the organization.

The first review is by the unit manager's boss. All the unit budgets for the boss's organization will have been consolidated to give the boss a first look at his or her overall budget. In this review, the unit manager is expected to explain, justify, and defend the submitted numbers. With the help of accounting, there are comparisons with the budgets of interacting organizations to check consistency.

When the boss has approved all subordinate budgets, the process is repeated at the next level. The boss's budget is transformed and consolidated with peer organizations to provide the budget for the manager at the next higher level. That manager then reviews the budgets of all his or her subordinates, and so on.

Each review may cause changes, which then have to be reflected back down the organization. This process can take months, and be full of surprises for all managers. They might believe, more than once, that their budgets have been approved, only to find expenses cut and/or outputs increased *again* as a result of higher management review.

This iterative process ends with final review (which might result in yet another round of changes) and approval of the total company budget by the board of directors. This board

It is always a mistake to assume budgets are unimportant. Even if higher management does not appear to emphasize them in your company, managers who miss budgets are handy scapegoats if big problems surface during the year.

review is typically held at the last board meeting before the new (budget) year begins. After board approval, the final budgets are distributed to all managers.

USES OF THE BUDGET BY HIGHER MANAGEMENT

The budget is useful to higher management in six basic ways:

1. *To implement strategy.* As said in Chapter 1, the budget is most fundamentally the company's plan (or actually the sum of all its plans) for next year. Therefore, the first use of the budget (during its preparation) is to implement the things that higher management wants to do—the company's strategy. The main purpose of all the budget reviews is to ensure that proper priorities are being given to the things higher management wants emphasized, and that the whole organization is going in the same direction.

2. *To coordinate all company work.* Also during budget preparation, higher management wants to ensure that the whole company is going in the same direction to implement the desired strategy. This is crucial for business success; for the music to be enjoyable, everyone has to sing off the same page.

3. *To predict results and needs.* Higher management needs adequate profit and cash flow to satisfy investors and fund what it wants to do. If the initial budget does not predict this, it almost certainly will be redone. Similarly, higher management needs to know the resources of all kinds needed to produce adequate results, so necessary resources can be obtained—people hired, equipment bought, money borrowed, and so forth.

4. *To keep score.* As the budget year unfolds, higher management uses comparison of actual results with the approved budget to answer the question, How well are we

doing? If company, department, or unit budgets are being significantly missed, managements are alerted to take corrective action. This may range from cost reductions to replacement of managers to changes in priorities and strategy. If budgets are being significantly beaten, managements are alerted to look at desirable opportunities that were considered unaffordable at budget preparation time.

5. *For control.* This and the following use affect unit managers most directly. Higher management uses the budget to control costs and activities. Some companies have outright prohibitions against overspending any budget, and most companies require special justification of any proposed activity that is not in the budget.

The approved budget is the unit manager's bible. There will be at least monthly review of results versus budget in many companies, and sometimes reference to it almost daily. Every change that comes up, and everything unit managers want to do, will be considered against the numbers in the budget. If their budgets are being met, they can expect relative peace. If budgets are being missed, managers should expect to have to explain and defend the variations, and to be required to develop corrective action. They may propose changes in work and costs that are logical in the light of changed conditions; however, if such changes violate the budget, their approval may be difficult to obtain.

6. *For measurement.* Using the budget to measure managers and their key people is a natural follow-up to using it to control costs and activities. Fortunately, it is not as simple as, "Beat your budget and you are a hero; miss your budget and you are a bum." The world changes and thus priorities and tasks change across the year, and actual results therefore may differ widely from the budget. However, unit managers must always realize that *they* are the ones who must call the attention of their bosses to the changed conditions and directions. They should never just sit back and say, "No problem, my boss knows why I am missing my budget."

Overall, then, we can say that the budget is used to:

- Implement strategy and coordinate work
- Plan, track, control, and measure performance
- Decide when objectives, strategies, priorities, plans, and/or personnel should be changed

CHAPTER 3

WHAT TO EXPECT AT BUDGET TIME

The announcement "It's budget time!" is never greeted with cheers.

One hopes that advance notice is given of the budgeting schedule, and that the start of budgeting is accompanied by:

- Company or division strategic guidance and priorities
- Detailed instructions regarding the budget forms and the budgeting process
- Common assumptions every unit should make

Some companies do all this. In other companies, some of this guidance is supplied by an informal memo or staff meeting discussion by the boss, or in a kickoff meeting featuring the boss and accounting. In still other companies, unit managers and their key people find out that budgeting has started only from the arrival of budget forms and meager instructions on their desks.

No matter how it starts, budget time in most companies is a frenzied time as managers and their key people struggle to predict what they will need, and what they can do, next year. They generally feel that they are not allotted enough time to do this, and often it seems that unit managers and their key people are doing nothing but budgeting for weeks. (You begin to wonder who is minding the store.)

The *work* of budgeting is planning next year's work and predicting important numerical results. For now, however, the specific tasks during budget time are:

1. Filling in the budget forms with next year's predicted results

2. Presenting that result to the boss and others
3. Redoing the budget forms in response to directions received at these presentations/reviews
4. Continuing this cycle until the final budget is approved

These tasks involve thinking, data gathering, negotiation, and meetings with bosses, accounting, peers, and your people.

COMPLETING THE BUDGET FORMS

Filling in the budget forms *properly* constitutes practically all the unit manager's work of budgeting, the subject of the rest of this book.

However, to get your feet wet in the subject now, let's illustrate what is involved in completing the simple payroll unit budget form shown in Chapter 1 (Figure 1 on page 5). In the process, we will introduce the concept of how to treat major, substantial, and minor costs. Phrases like "plan and analyze next year's work" and "estimate the changes" are hints about the budgeting work to be done, treatment of which starts in Chapter 4.

Here is the example process of filling out the payroll budget form.

Salaries

First list the names of current employees. Their monthly salaries for next year are their current salaries (from your payroll information) plus any planned raise for the months after that raise is given. To simplify the arithmetic, assume raises are given on the first day of a month.

Some companies require salary planning to be done before budgeting, and planned raises are obtained from that. Other companies may specify an average raise, to be budgeted for all employees, say, on July 1.

If you are given no direction,

1. Use current salaries after the names.
2. Predict that the average raise will be the same as this year's average (obtain this from accounting).
3. Add a line called "Salary Raises" and put total predicted raises, spread evenly across the year, on that line.

This avoids predicting ahead of time how well different people will perform and therefore what raise each will get, and also avoids writing down specific raise information that you would not want your people to see.

Next, you have to analyze your workload and predict whether you need more or fewer people. If you need more people, add one or more "New Hire" entries to the list of employees' names. Forecast the month you will hire them and the monthly salary they will be paid (perhaps with help from human resources), and enter the salary numbers in the appropriate months.

If you know a person is leaving and the date, end their salary in that month. If you need fewer people, or have been told to reduce people, you have to predict which ones will be let go and when, and remove their salary entries after that date. (You can avoid being so specific by including all employees' salaries for the whole year and adding a general line called "Salary Reductions," but you still would not want your people to see such an item.)

Fringe Benefits

These are costs of medical insurance and the like. These are predicted based on a mathematical formula developed by accounting. The right numbers to enter cannot be known by unit managers. Either accounting makes these monthly entries, based on the manager's salary numbers, or accounting gives the formula to unit managers and they do the calculation.

**Use per-
spective on
budget line
item en-
tries. If a
particular
line item is
only 2 per-
cent of
your total
budget,
don't spend
much time
on it.**

Other Indirect Costs

These are nonsalary costs that cannot be related directly to production of revenue. Different companies line-itemize them in different ways. Almost all companies include an "Other" line, in which all nonitemized other indirect costs must be entered. Examples of other indirect costs that may be itemized on other budget forms are freight, real estate taxes, utilities, advertising, maintenance and repair, and equipment depreciation.

How do you predict these other indirect costs? That depends on whether a particular expense is a minor or major amount relative to your total budget, or in between (which we will call "substantial"). For your unit, you either know this intuitively or base it on this year's actual costs or on known plans for next year. (Or you may learn in the process of budgeting that what you thought would be "substantial" in fact will be "major," requiring you to change your approach to predicting it.)

Let's take travel and living (meaning hotel, restaurant, and other living expense associated with travel) as an example. You have to analyze how much travel your unit will have to do, how much each trip or an average trip will cost the company, and when the trips will be taken. If travel will be infrequent, a *minor expense*, quickly estimate the number of trips, the average cost per trip (obtained from experience, accounting, or a travel agent), multiply the two together, and enter at estimated times.

If travel and living is a *major expense*, you must plan and analyze next year's work, predict how many trips to what locations will be required and when, and use travel industry data and personal experience to estimate the cost of each trip. The numerical results of this analysis are then entered in the appropriate months on the budget form.

In most cases, travel and living is a *substantial expense*, neither negligible nor a major piece of the total budget. If so:

- Start with this year's actual travel and living cost, obtained from your monthly financial report or otherwise from accounting.
- Think about what will change next year (for example, having to serve a newly acquired, remotely located subsidiary will probably require more travel).
- If you think nothing will change significantly, use this year's actual costs for next year.
- If you expect significant changes, estimate the amount of the changes (perhaps as a percentage of this year's costs), and add it to this year's actual costs to get next year's total.
- Unless there will be very few trips or there is a known travel peak time, spread the costs thus predicted evenly over the months of next year.

Most other indirect costs can be budgeted by determining by whether they are minor, substantial, or major. For example, if telephone expense is:

- *Minor,* just use this year's actual amounts
- *Substantial,* obtain this year's actual costs for your unit, think about what will change next year (more people mean more phones and perhaps more calls, new interaction with a remote location means more long distance calls, etc.), and build and spread the cost amounts accordingly
- *Major* (as it might be for a recruiting function, for example), you must plan and analyze how many phones, how many long-distance calls per month per employee plus location and duration, and you must predict peaks and valleys of activity

Exceptions are other indirect costs that are composed of only a few, but large, charges. An example in the payroll budget form would be the use of an outside accounting firm to figure payroll taxes (budgeted under "Outside Services"). For such large individual costs, you should get a quotation or estimate from the vendor or use one of the other ways of estimating costs discussed in Chapter 9.

Finally, all other indirect expense not included in the itemization must be entered on the "Other" line. In a good budgeting system, the major and substantial costs are itemized, so "Other" is a minor cost. In that case, you don't have to figure out all the various kinds of costs involved; you just predict using this year's actual and expected changes in total "Other." If, however, the "Other" category is major in your company, you have to break it into significant items yourself, and apply the above techniques to these items.

Supplemental Information

This example budget form calls for two kinds of supplemental information: "New Hires" and "Computer Time (Hours)." (They are probably there to help human resources and data processing plan their work and necessary resources.) The former is filled in directly from the "Salaries" entry; you previously determined whether you need more people by analyzing next year's anticipated workload.

Rework, time pressure, and emotion are inherent in budgeting. We can't guarantee to remove them, but the remaining chapters of this book will show you how to minimize them.

To predict computer time, you need data processing's help. (This help should be easy to get because data processing needs your computer requirements to do *its* budget.) Computer time needed to serve the payroll unit depends on the number of employees, frequency of paychecks, and such things as the extent and complexity of payroll calculations and printing. Give these types of information to data processing and ask for, and use, its estimate of needed computer time. Even if payroll work won't change next year, computer hardware and software may be modified, changing the computer time needed to process payroll, so you need data processing's input in any case.

THE BUDGETING CLIMATE

We have already mentioned several times that there is a lot of rework associated with budgeting—that every review may cause all unit budgets to be redone *again*. There are two other almost universal aspects of the climate that surrounds budgeting—time pressure and emotion—that we should discuss as part of what to expect at budget time.

Time Pressure

The time pressure for unit managers is of the "hurry up and wait" variety. Boards of directors generally approve budgets in December for the following year. The amount of work required and the multiple levels of organization usually mean that the budgeting process starts no later than September. And probably only one or two weeks are allowed for each step.

Thus in September unit managers are asked to predict all their costs and outputs for the period that is three to fifteen months away and to accomplish this in two weeks or less. Bosses may throw the forms back to be redone—quickly, quickly—at the first review. Then there is a wait until the boss's budget is reviewed and then probably another modification—quickly, quickly. And so on.

Unfortunately, many budgeting processes can be described by the old adage "There is never enough time to do it right, but always time to do it over." Since they have to get all their regular work done as well, unit managers seldom have the time for the analysis and reflection that their plans for next year merit. So expect some long nights and weekends at budget time; they will come in spurts, often unpredictably.

Emotion

Emotion partly results from the time pressure, but there is more to it than that. Remember that your boss is both a *reviewer* of your budget and a *submitter* of his or her own budget, which also has to get approved. In one way, budgeting is a multidimensional guessing game—about the future, about the success and costs of planned projects, and about what the reviewer will accept (and, from the reviewer's point of view, what the submitter can accomplish). You and your boss know that both of you will be measured heavily on your actual results versus this guessing game.

Is it any wonder that you, your people, your boss, and his or her boss may get emotional in the midst of all this? There are so many "can so, cannot" discussions involved in budget reviews. You say project A will take ten people, and your boss says you can do it with eight. You feel overworked and understaffed, and your boss insists that you cut costs 10 percent from this year (at least partly because his or her boss demanded it).

The key in this emotional climate is to determine what are the real problems and what are just "noise" in the emotional confusion. A grumpy boss at budget time is normal. Depending on his or her personality, you have to judge whether a sarcastic remark on how "luxurious" your plans are is a real criticism or just an emotional reaction to pressure. What you have to do is:

- Get to know and understand your boss (which you should do anyway).
- Submit a budget that is intelligent, rational, and responsive.
- Defend it vigorously and objectively.
- If the boss persists after such defense, the problem is real, so switch from defense to responsiveness, enlisting his or her guidance in modifying your budget.

If the budget you submit is three times what the boss expected, you are almost guaranteed an emotional reaction. Communicate, communicate, well in advance.

GENERAL BUDGETING TIPS

Let's wrap up our general discussion of budget time with some tips that can make life easier.

• *Keep careful notes of the assumptions, reasoning, and calculations behind your budget submission.* Weeks later, when a particular number is attacked in a new review, you may not remember how you arrived at that number.

• *Put your budgeting form on a personal computer spreadsheet.* This makes it easier to track each revision and the reasoning behind it. If done right, it also eliminates arithmetic and multiple-entry errors. Most budgets involve the manipulation of a lot of numbers; don't underestimate the potential for embarrassing arithmetic mistakes. Also, many budgets require a number to be reentered and used in another part of the form or another form.

Take the time and trouble to program the spreadsheet so that all such transfers are automatically made by the computer. If you don't, you may forget one or more entries of a certain number in a subsequent modification, making hash of your budget totals. For example, if the payroll budget form is done manually, you might forget to change fringe benefits if you have to change salaries; on a properly designed spreadsheet, fringe benefits would be changed automatically if salaries change.

• *Absent other information about your boss, expect the costs in your first submission to be cut*, and understand that the first cut may not be the last. Therefore, do not cut them to the bone yourself in your first submission.

If your costs are cut beyond what you believe is required to do the expected job, don't be shy. Make sure your boss knows you believe this; you are going to be measured against this budget, after all.

• *Remember that precision is not accuracy*. If all you can really predict about telephone costs next year is that they will be between $2,000 and $2,500, there is no value in putting $2,378 in the budget. In fact, it is harmful, because the four figures mislead by implying more knowledge than you have. In such a case, please put $2,400 in your budget.

CHAPTER 4

THE UNIT MANAGER'S
WORK OF BUDGETING

New budgeters tend to think that there is some magic way to generate good budgets, but the only magic is in the principles and techniques, hard work, knowledge, and intelligence.

OK, so it is budget time. The budget forms have arrived on your desk, and you have been told to submit the unit's budget in two weeks. Or, if you are not the unit manager, you have been asked to budget your part of the unit's work. One hopes you have been given extensive guidance, but perhaps not (see the box at the end of this chapter). What do you do?

The simple illustration of completing the payroll budget form in Chapter 3 only scratches the surface. A function like payroll probably does not change much year to year, and the illustration still left some questions up in the air about how to generate certain budget numbers. We have to answer those questions, particularly for units whose specific work content changes every year.

To decide what has to be done, you first have to understand what is required from budgeting.

THE REQUIRED RESULTS OF BUDGETING

As noted in Chapter 1, all unit managers are required to predict their units' costs for next year. Some managers have to forecast the outputs that can be achieved: revenue, shipments, assemblies, transactions, service repair calls, and the like. Many managers also have to supply supplemental forecasts of various kinds.

Now no unit exists in a vacuum, self-contained in its work. All units need inputs and support *from* other organizational elements, and all units supply outputs *to* other organizational elements that those functions need as inputs and support for their work. In a factory, the shipping function is the only one that has outputs direct to the customer; all other factory units hand their outputs to other internal organizations. Thus, another important result of budgeting is each unit's definition of its needs from, and outputs to, other organizational elements within the company. This is required to ensure that the whole company is going in the same direction to carry out the desired strategy.

Thus, what is required from unit managers in budgeting is to generate good predictions for next year of:

- Expected costs
- Achievable outputs
- Requested supplemental information
- Needs from, and outputs to, other organizational elements within the company

ACHIEVABLE OUTPUTS

One of the results of budgeting is *achievable outputs,* which may or may not be the same as *required outputs.* A factory assembly unit may be told that 3,000 widgets are needed next year. If, after diligent analysis, the unit manager believes that only 2,500 units can be produced, 2,500 is the number that should go into the budget. Higher management wants the best prediction possible; if the forecast is not satisfactory, resources can be added or redirected or plans changed. No one's interests are served if the requested number of assemblies is just parroted back in the budget with no hope of accomplishment.

PLANNING THE UNIT'S WORK

To supply these required budgeting outputs or results, unit managers and their key people must first answer a whole set of questions:

> What are we expected to accomplish?
>
> How are we going to accomplish it? (That is, what processes and activities are going to be involved in getting our work done?)
>
> What inputs and support do we need, and can we get, from other organizations within and outside the company?
>
> What kinds of effort, purchases, services, and costs are involved in getting our work done?
>
> How do I know everything you are telling me won't change as the year moves along?

What have we just said? We have said that *unit managers first have to plan their unit's work for next year.* This is the first component of the unit manager's work of budgeting.

We will discuss what a plan is at greater length in Chapter 7. For now, we can say that a plan tells how you are going to get from point A to point B. In business plans in general, point A is the set of resources, skills, processes, and working environment that your unit now possesses, and point B is the set of things that need to be accomplished. For the budget, point B is the set of things to be accomplished *next year.*

Planning the work requires that the unit's work must first be understood, so a prerequisite is *defining the unit's work.* This takes effort, but it is effort that managers should expend anyway, just to do their jobs. Defining the work is more complex than it may seem, so Chapter 6 is devoted to the right way to define the unit's work.

Once the work is defined and understood, the outputs expected of the unit over the next year, with the required schedule, must be identified. Similarly, the kinds and amounts of inputs and support that will be available, and when, must be determined. Then, how you are going to do the work must be decided. This is all discussed in Chapter 7.

The joker in this work planning is the inherent uncertainty of the future, reflected in the last question in the series at the beginning of this section. However, as explained in Chapter 1 in the box on page 7, the uncertainty makes the planning more important, not less. The uncertainty cannot be avoided—future uncertainty is not resolved until time passage makes the future the present—but it can be handled and its effects minimized. Future uncertainty looms so large in budgeting that handling it is covered next, in Chapter 5.

GENERATING THE NUMBERS

All the planning work goes for nought if you predict the output and cost numbers poorly. For example, you can be perfect in thinking through every single step involved in painting a house; however, if your estimates of the amount of paint needed and the time required are way off, your cost estimate will be worthless.

Generating the budget numbers properly is the second component of the unit manager's work of budgeting. In reality, of course, the work of generating these numbers is not divorced from the planning work of budgeting. Indeed, predicting the numbers is the result, and the natural last step, of the planning. However, it is appropriate to discuss number generation separately, because there is a right way and a number of wrong ways to choose the numbers that actually go into the budget. In the house-painting example, the right way to estimate labor would be to plan all the steps—cleaning, spackling, walls, trim, etc.—and estimate each from experience. A wrong way could be to base labor hours on total square feet without regard for the particular preparation required.

Chapter 8 discusses how to generate the budget numbers in general. Because cost estimating is so large a part of budgeting, it is treated separately in Chapter 9.

MAKING ESTIMATES

Are you basically uncomfortable making estimates? Some people are. Do you resist putting numbers down until you have complete information? Some people do. However, companies and their managers need to plan for the future, and need to predict the consequences of those plans so they can choose the best plans for next year. Making uncertain estimates and predictions is central to management and budgeting work, so budgeters must get comfortable with the idea of dealing with those uncertainties. If you find it hard to be comfortable, remember that part of your problem is just your state of mind. Given that businesses need predictions, seeking certainty is an illusion in any case. Only when an event has happened and you are recording history will you find certainty. And, if business prediction were simple, they could replace you with a high school kid, right?

The other part of getting comfortable with predictions is to make them in the way that results in the most probable prediction possible. The first step is defining and planning the work, covered in Chapters 6 and 7. The rest is using the best principles and techniques to put numerical values on the results of the planning, the subject of Chapters 8 and 9.

GETTING THE RIGHT BUDGET APPROVED

Obviously, developing good budgets is of no benefit if managers cannot get them approved. While expressed as numbers of dollars for different kinds of costs and outputs, budget approval really means the acceptance and authorization of your plans for next year, including:

- Expected and committed results
- Resources required to achieve the results
- Needed capital investments
- Action programs to generate outputs, improve performance, and reduce costs
- Support and inputs required from other organizational elements

Getting the right budget approved is not a trivial task. It is a selling job—the "customers" being the bosses—involving a set of objective and subjective factors like any other selling job. It requires the same amount of energy and focus that must be applied to the rest of the work of budgeting. Therefore, it is the third major component of the unit manager's work of budgeting, and Chapter 11 is devoted to it.

Every manager's particular budgeting problems are unique. However, the right principles, techniques, and practices can be applied beneficially in every company.

CONCLUSION

This then is the unit manager's work of budgeting:

- Planning the unit's work for next year
- Generating the cost and other numbers that go into the budget submission
- Selling the budget so that the right budget gets approved

Our concern is that unit managers get approval of budgets that give them the resources they need to accomplish what is expected of them. Thus we need not be concerned with budgeting theories: nor do we need to become experts in accounting, investment analysis, or the like. What we need is more insight into this work of budgeting:

- Chapter 5 discusses how to handle the ever present uncertainty in budgeting.
- Chapter 6 shows how to define the unit's work, which is the prerequisite for planning for next year.
- Chapter 7 discusses how to plan next year's work.
- Chapter 8 describes how to generate the numbers that go into your budget.
- Chapter 9 treats cost estimating, by far the most common budget numbers that have to be generated.
- Chapter 10 shows you how to put all this work together in an efficient process.
- Chapter 11 describes the all–important final step: selling your budget and getting the right budget approved.

PREBUDGETING ACTIVITY

At some enlightened companies, higher management specifies "what," in terms of goals, strategies, priorities, and problems for concentrated attention. They rely on the rest of the managers and their key people to decide "how" to carry out their wishes, and "how much" it will cost and use scarce resources. Therefore, before budgeting starts, higher management actively directs the identification of critical factors for success, problems, and desired improvements. It also communicates preliminary budget targets that will constitute satisfactory performance.

If you work for an enlightened company, be thankful, because your budgeting work is a lot easier. All managers at such companies begin their budgets with good knowledge of what the company wants to do next year, what is generally expected of them, and what top management's priorities are.

Unfortunately, many companies are closer to the opposite extreme. Unit managers learn that the budgeting process has begun when forms arrive at their desk. The forms are accompanied by a letter from accounting giving a few ground rules (such as "assume salary increases average 5 percent") and stating that the manager's budget numbers are due back to accounting in a week or two. There is also a pep talk letter from the controller noting the importance of minimizing costs next year. Needless to say, managers in these companies have to be creative to figure out what higher management wants. The planning element of their budgeting work is particularly important: Unit managers need a coherent, logical framework to defend their budget submissions. Such a framework lets them understand cause and effect, the parts of their budget submission that will be changed by requirements different from what they assumed. Thus the changes that probably will flow from the budget reviews will be easier to accomplish.

CHAPTER 5

HANDLING UNCERTAINTY

Managers live and work in the future, and the future is always uncertain. Beyond that, many factors that have important effects on their organizations are uncontrollable.

The biggest difficulty in developing budgets is the fact that the future is always uncertain. You can't get rid of this uncertainty by doing more work or crunching more numbers. Nor will spending an extra month on the budget really help. That will only reduce the time element of uncertainty by a month out of a prediction time of more than twelve months. As for starting the budget later, that will only make your preparation more frantic, because it still has to be finished before the budget year begins, a minimum prediction time of twelve months.

This uncertainty permeates all aspects of budgeting, so it makes sense to discuss how to handle it before proceeding to the rest of our subjects.

KINDS OF UNCERTAINTY IN BUDGETING

The simplest kind of uncertainty is temporary uncertainty, meaning information known by someone in the company but not communicated to you in time for budget submission. Typical examples are the number of each product that will have to be produced, what responsibilities your unit will have toward a new remote location, and the specific territory to be covered by a sales branch. This kind of uncertainty is really only lack of communication. The solution for it is simply to dig out the information, seeking whatever help you need to find it.

Then there is normal planning uncertainty; for example, you are probably not certain of your labor costs for a particular project you have to forecast for next year. This kind of uncertainty is tackled by knowledge, capability, and experience. Unit managers and their key people get paid partly to plan things well, and Chapters 5 through 10 will help.

The type of uncertainty that makes budgeting so difficult can be called *inherent uncertainty*. That is, no matter how smart and experienced you are, you cannot predict such things as interest rates, particular customer decisions, commodity prices, and the like. (If the experts are often wrong in predicting interest rates, how can we expect to predict them correctly?)

There are two kinds of inherent uncertainty for a unit manager:

1. Every company has *external* factors that have important effects on their results—various industry, market, economic, government, and financial factors.
2. All unit managers also face *internal* company factors that strongly affect their costs and outputs. These are things dictated in other parts of the company and beyond their own control. Examples are purchasing and personnel policies, employee benefit levels, production schedules, marketing priorities, and the like.

The distinction between external and internal factors is real, but both are handled the same way. The key to each is that they are *uncontrollable* by the unit manager whose budget they affect. A purchasing unit's workload is affected both by the economy—boom times make prompt material delivery more difficult, for example—and by the company's production needs, neither of which the purchasing manager can influence.

The inherent uncertainties are our prime concerns; temporary and planning uncertainties can be resolved by good work, while the inherent uncertainties won't go away until the future becomes the present.

EXPLICIT ASSUMPTIONS

How is this inherent uncertainty ordinarily handled? You can get advice from bosses, experts, and your favorite media prophet, and knowledge and experience help. But let's face it—the only thing you can do about an inherent uncertainty is to guess. (The bosses, experts, and the media prophet are guessing, too.) That is, you *make an assumption* about what will happen or about the cost, price, or value of an important item in next year's budget.

The problem is that most budgeters make "implicit" assumptions. That is, they are never identified as assumptions but just carried along with the cost and other numbers that are developed. Then, midway through the year, if the budget is being missed, no one remembers any assumptions, they just focus on the fact that the budget is being missed.

The right way to do it is to make *explicit assumptions*. The guesses made about important uncertainties are prominently noted when made. They are then carried along with the budget numbers (as supplementary information with the budget forms) throughout the review and approval process. All the budget planning and numbers are made consistent with the assumptions, and are changed if the assumptions change.

An Illustration

Consider a unit manager responsible for publishing timetables in a commuter bus company. In the past, company bus schedules were stable and new timetables were published only twice a year. This year, however, frequent schedule changes made by higher management have required the publishing of six new timetables. As a result, this unit manager's current year budget is being badly missed.

No one is certain how many changes to expect next year; how should she budget? The answer is that she has to guess whether the new instability will continue or whether things will go back to normal. Chances are that she will be wrong, whichever way she guesses, because she has no control over the schedule changes the bus company makes (an *internal* uncertainty).

If she implicitly (that is, in her own head, telling nobody) assumes two timetables must be published next year, her budget will be missed again if she has to do more than two. If she implicitly assumes six, like this year, her bosses will say her budget is too high. She will be told to redo the budget, cutting costs.

On the other hand, if she announces the number of publishings as an explicit assumption and includes that assumption with her budget submission (for example, "New timetables will be published twice during the year, in March and September") at least two good things will happen. First, her bosses will be made aware of an inherent uncertainty in her costs and be reminded of another cost that their decisions on schedule changes will affect. Second, attention and measurement will focus (at budget time and throughout the year) on her cost for a given amount of publishing. Minimizing cost per publishing, as well as ensuring accuracy and timeliness, is what she is paid to do—what she can control.

Explicit assumptions in budgeting also yield an incidental benefit on temporary uncertainty. An explicit assumption will almost surely expedite the provision of the needed information to you.

Benefits of Explicit Assumptions

The emotional climate of budgeting mostly arises out of the uncertainty of the future. Explicit assumptions are an antidote for emotion. They do away with statements by your boss like, "You won't need five more people because next year's economy is going to be poor." You and your boss can first rationally discuss your assumptions, and simply change them to your boss's preference if there is disagreement. Then the two of you can focus on your costs and outputs— the proper subject for budget discussions—under the assumed conditions. You can avoid the psychological games of (*You*) "I have to pad my budget to handle all the uncertainty," and (*Boss*) "I have to find where he or she is sandbagging the budget." Instead, the discussion becomes (*Both*) "Given the assumed conditions, how can we maximize unit output and minimize unit cost?"

There are other benefits. All management is made to realize better how decisions made in one part of the company will affect other parts. Distinguishing the "external uncontrollables" allows management to understand and focus on the controllable factors—the things that it can influence and change. Explicit assumptions also make for fairer measurement: The publishing unit manager in the bus company should not be measured on how well she guesses what the total amount of publishing will be. Finally, morale and performance are improved; you don't mind taking on a challenge if convinced that the boss understands the problems and will measure you fairly, right?

MAKING USEFUL BUDGETING ASSUMPTIONS

Making proper budgeting assumptions is not a trivial task. If you start with a general assumption like "Inflation will be 3 percent next year," you still have to reason through how such an inflation rate will affect your unit's costs.

At the other extreme, your bosses will not let you get away with an assumption like "We will reduce our costs 15 percent next year." Such a statement baldly assumes that you will do your job, part of which is exactly to manage and reduce costs. Higher management wants to know how you will do that, not to have success at cost reduction just assumed.

The right way to select the proper subjects for budgeting assumptions is an inside-out reasoning process. Don't start with generalities like inflation or recession; you won't know how to apply the assumption after you make it. Start with the definition (Chapter 6) and planning (Chapter 7) of the unit's work. From this, decide the most important factors that determine and influence unit outputs and costs. Then decide which of these output dictators and cost drivers are inherently uncertain (that is, uncontrollable). These are the subjects for which assumptions then are made.

Some examples of inherent uncertainties that may have major effects on costs and outputs of various functions, and thus are appropriate subjects for budgeting assumptions, are the following:

Payroll Unit	Number of time card errors
	Government payroll tax regulation changes
	New operations in new states (requiring new payroll tax structures)
Machine Shop	The price of raw stock
	Toxic waste handling regulations
	Wage rates (set by human resources)
Sales Unit	"Make" or "buy" policy changes by customers
	Bankruptcy of a major customer
	Whether a new product can be delivered on schedule by the factory
Bank Branch	Interest rates
	New competitor offering better terms
	Status (layoffs? moving?) of major businesses in the branch's area
Factory Assembly Unit	Prices of purchased components
	Number of engineering change notices per product
	Wage rates
	Environmental regulations

A caution is that assumptions are not appropriate for things to which managers are supposed to contribute. For example, an assembly unit manager is supposed to contribute to the factory production schedule. Thus, such unit managers cannot claim that the production schedule is inherently uncertain, even though they cannot control it themselves, because they are *involved* in establishing it. On the other hand, factory wage levels set by human resources—a different department—are a valid example of an important uncontrollable cost for an assembly unit manager.

Once this selection of the subjects for the assumptions is done, the numerical values—"Prices of components A, B, and C will increase 15 percent over this year; other component prices will stay the same"—or descriptive statements— "Business X will move its factory out of our area during the spring"—are simply your most reasonable expectations based on knowledge, experience, and thought.

Possible assumptions for the example payroll unit are the following:

- "Time card errors requiring manual adjustment will continue to average 200 per month."
- "Withholding tax regulations will not change during the year, while Social Security and Medicare tax changes will be limited to those already known."
- "This payroll unit will not be given responsibility for any new remotely located operations during the year."

How important is it that our assumptions turn out to be correct? It is important that the assumptions that influence management action be reasonable, but correctness is not the point. *The reason explicit assumptions are used is that the budget must deal with future uncertainty about uncontrollable things.* If the numerical value of the assumption proves incorrect, that alerts management to the fact that conditions are then different from what was predicted, so they must react by changing actions and expectations. This identification of uncontrollables and the use of assumptions in managing and measuring are the important things, not whether the initial assumptions were correct.

SELLING THE IDEA OF EXPLICIT ASSUMPTIONS

Some companies make explicit assumptions an integral part of the budgeting process. Selection of assumption subjects

Make sure you work hard at continual performance improvements on factors that are under the unit's control. Besides being your job, this guards against your being considered a whiner for putting so much emphasis on things that are uncontrollable.

and values is done early, with direct higher-management involvement so that assumptions are consistent across the company or division. Budget reviews at all levels then focus separately on the assumptions and on how the company should employ its resources. As the budget year progresses, assumptions are modified when changes in external or internal factors invalidate an assumption, and these modifications are reflected in measurement of performance against budgets.

If your company does not include explicit assumptions in its budgeting process, unit managers and their key people should still make them. Their task is more difficult, however,

---

THE ASSUMPTIONS PROCESS

1. Think through the unit's work definition and plans and select subjects for assumptions as explained in the previous section. (There will be only a small number of truly important inherent uncertainties, but these can be crucial.)
2. Make reasonable predictions for assumption values for each subject.
3. Submit these prominently as supplementary information included in the submitted budget forms.
4. In budget presentations and reviews, stress the relationship and influence of your assumptions on your various budget numbers.
5. If your boss wants an assumption changed, do it without argument. However, if challenged, vigorously defend the uncontrollability of your assumption subjects.
6. Throughout the year at performance reviews, stress how variation in values of uncontrollables have affected your costs and outputs.

because they have to sell their bosses on the value of explicit assumptions in budgeting, management, and measurement. What they need to sell are that:

- Particular important things about the unit's work are uncontrollable by the unit.
- Unit costs and outputs may be significantly changed by changes in such inherent uncertainties (in other words, the score may be different if the rules change).
- Continual reference to, and review of, explicit assumptions is the best way to handle these inherent uncertainties.
- Unit managers and their key people should be measured on how well they manage and perform on the factors they *can* influence and control.

It's multiple-choice time again. Unit managers usually control so little of their destiny that they often feel they are just reacting to events designed to complicate their lives. Some of that is unavoidable. But after going through this assumptions process:

a. Management performance will improve, and the job will be more enjoyable.
b. Unit managers and their key people, and presumably the boss, will understand their jobs better—that is, what is controllable and uncontrollable—and will be able to focus their energy on things that they *can* change.
c. They can achieve the best budget possible under the circumstances.
d. They will be better prepared to handle the unpleasant surprises that come every year.
e. All of the above.

The right answer is emphatically e.

CHAPTER 6

DEFINING THE UNIT'S WORK

Definition of the unit's work should be done before budgeting begins, because the ever present time pressure will make it difficult to accomplish during budgeting.

Unit managers and their key people must understand their unit's work, not only for budgeting, but to be able to manage that work. The work definition is usually more complex than it first appears, and requires some effort.

The proper way to define the unit's work is in terms of its outputs, inputs, and activities. Visualize your unit's work in terms of the following flowchart:

Outputs are the physical or informational things that the unit produces—product designs, assembled units, reports, paychecks, and so on. *Inputs* are the "raw material," instructions, and the like, that are supplied to the unit to do its work. *Activities* are what the unit *does* to transform inputs into outputs.

Most of a unit's outputs go to other units, and most of its inputs are outputs from other units. Further, different choices of activities change the inputs required. Thus outputs, inputs, and activities are the nuts and bolts of how different units and functions work together to conduct the business, and the place where performance improvements and cost reductions are made. For a payroll unit, automation of time records (that is, different inputs) would eliminate or

45

Most problems are interfunctional, and most progress can usually be made by finding better ways to do things *across* units and functions— that is, by changing outputs and inputs as well as activities.

change review, data entry, and error correction activities. Similarly, the activity change of switching to an external payroll service would change most of the inputs that the payroll unit requires.

Each unit's work definition is different, of course, so you have to determine your own. However, this chapter will show you how.

ACTIVITIES

Let's start with activities. People tend to talk in terms of functions ("I am in sales"), but discussion in activity terms ("I make cold calls and sales presentations on products A, B, and C throughout Ohio") gives a better basis for managing the work, improving performance, predicting costs, and reducing costs. Thus, a focus on activities is the best way to define the work.

An activity is the way a business employs its resources (labor, materials, time, information, and technology) to produce particular outputs. For example, material flow in a factory can be discussed in terms of the functions involved: possibly material management, quality control, and accounting. However, those words don't tell you what you have to *do*. Much more information for managing and budgeting is contained in descriptions of the activities involved: Receive material, inspect material, move material, store material, pay for material, and supply material to assembly.

The activities a unit performs are determined by:

- Its required outputs
- Management decisions regarding equipment, people, processes, and procedures
- Inputs

Activities usually fall into a sort of hierarchy. In defining them, choose the level that is useful in managing and that involves significant costs. "Prepare reports" can be viewed as including the subsidiary activities of "creating reports" and "typing reports." These would be significant for a word processing unit, but not for an engineering function. The engineering unit may even consider "preparing reports" not worth identifying. That is, the engineering unit manager may decide to focus on activities like "design products," "modify products," and "maintain configuration control," and consider preparation of reports only an incidental part of each.

Further, the principle of diminishing returns applies to definition of activities. The important thing is to define high-cost and highly variable activities, and to relate them to outputs. An "other" category is useful and permissible for support and incidental activities that do not vary much with output. Every organization should also have something like "administration" to cover activities like training, appraisals, and employee communication.

OUTPUTS

Revenue is not properly an organizational output. In the sense of the work to be done, revenue is a by-product of outputs such as products shipped and services delivered.

There are many types of business organizations with many kinds of outputs. The *primary outputs* usually follow directly from the organization's function: assembled products from an assembly unit, orders from a sales unit, paychecks from a payroll unit, customers served from a restaurant operation, copies from a reproduction center, and products shipped from a division.

The next step must be the *specifications* that complete the description of the primary outputs. For the assembly unit, this includes specifications of the products assembled and the required quality level. For the sales unit, it includes the products sold and the geographical area or market in which they are sold. The paychecks from the payroll unit must be on time and correct in gross amounts, deductions, and net amounts. And so on.

Beyond these primary outputs, every organization has *information outputs*. The assembly unit must provide time records by project for its personnel, records of output achieved, and reports of usage and storage of toxic materials. The sales unit must report its sales calls and submit travel expense reports. The payroll unit must prepare and submit payroll tax returns. Plans, budgets, material requests, and such are required from most units.

Most organizations also have what we can call *service outputs*. They must satisfy inquiries and complaints, provide expertise to sister organizations in solution of problems, and the like. Sales, factory, and service people all have expert advice to give on design and features of new products. A reproduction center's primary output—copies—is a "service," but its service output is advice on what is possible, best, and most cost-effective in reproducing documents.

Ordinarily, the primary outputs are the main determinants of activities and costs, but not always. In some cases, information outputs—compliance with federal environmental, safety, and tax regulations—can add considerable effort and cost. Important outputs are not necessarily only the obvious ones, which is why deliberate analysis and observation are needed.

INPUTS

There are essentially three kinds of organizational inputs.

1. There are the things on which the organization operates, which we will call the *material*. These are the things that are traditionally considered inputs to any activity in the narrow definition of the term. For an assembly unit it is the material to be assembled, for an engineering function a new product requirement or a problem to be solved, for payroll it is the time records.

2. There are things from other functions that help an organization conduct its activities. These are the *tools*, assistance or support. Examples are computer programs, candidates for employment from human resources, artwork, and physical tools and equipment.

3. There are things that prescribe how an organization will do its work, the *instructions*. Examples are drawings, data entry procedures, bills of material, and policies and procedures.

Consider a sales unit. Its material inputs are the products and services to be sold and identification of current customers. Tool inputs can be advertising and sales promotion, proposals and quotations prepared by engineering, management visits, financing arrangements, and contract forms. Instructions include price lists and allowable terms and conditions, antitrust policies, order-entry procedures, and expense account rules for entertaining customers.

The material inputs can be physical things, such as component parts for assembly, faulty equipment for maintenance service, cash for a banking transaction, and the goods to be sold in a retail store. It can also be information, evidenced by paper or bits stored in a computer. Information is probably the more common input to business organizations: all the activity records that are accounting's inputs, product descriptions for sales, product requirements for engineering, material requests for purchasing, signed applications for insurance rating and pricing, and so forth. In the same way, tools can be physical things or information. Instructions are always information.

OUTPUT DICTATORS

OK, we have outputs, inputs, and activities, but we are not finished yet! To complete the definition of the unit's work, managers must understand what dictates their outputs and what causes or drives their costs (covered in the next section).

Once an organization's outputs are defined, the next task is to determine what dictates those outputs, so that you will know where to look for the numbers that define next year's budget.

Some organizations have outputs dictated directly by orders, contracts, or *revenue*. Examples are an engineering organization totally devoted to customer development contracts, a service function devoted to customer maintenance contracts, and most sales organizations.

More typical are organization outputs that are dictated by *derivatives of revenue*. Factories generally have a planning function that schedules all factory operations. Assembly, test, and machine shop organizations have their outputs defined by these schedules, rather than directly by revenue. For organizations whose transactions generate revenue—cashing checks, selling a security, or switching telephone calls—the transaction itself is the output that determines the work, rather than the revenue involved.

The next logical category is *outside requirements*, independent of revenue. Legal and regulatory requirements, markets, and competition all dictate company outputs, for example, annual and quarterly reports, compliance with environmental regulations, proposal information that satisfies government procurement regulations, and special services provided to match competitors.

Some outputs are dictated by *structural factors*. These dictators are a result of the physical, procedural, and organizational way in which the company does business. The way a company is organized fundamentally establishes the responsibilities and outputs of all its units. The fact of locations in a number of states and countries dictates a particular set of shipping, tax return, and communication outputs.

Finally, there are units whose outputs are dictated by *requests for service*. Their outputs are determined simply by the demands of their "customers," and they might be called "level of effort" functions. Reproduction, word processing, art departments, and parts of facilities are examples of such functions.

In practice, one organization may have outputs of all the above types. A purchasing unit in a manufacturing department can have outputs dictated by pass-through revenue, production schedules, and inventory policy; an outside requirement to report on the proportion of orders placed with

The most important use of the knowledge of cost drivers is not in budgeting but in improving organizational performance. The cost drivers show where to look for the biggest improvement payoffs.

small or minority businesses; and a service requirement to fulfill random headquarters purchasing needs.

COST DRIVERS

The things that cause or drive the unit's costs must be understood for the unit's work to be planned and budgeted intelligently. Knowledge of cost drivers is also important in evaluating changes during the budgeting process, and also changes in plans during the course of the budget year. That knowledge allows managers to understand quickly whether such changes will have major or minor effects, whether they require quick reaction or can be taken in stride.

Required outputs and output dictators are obvious cost drivers. Usually, the more products assembled or engineering changes to be made and processed, the higher will be the costs. Also, output complexity and diversity increases costs. Changing output requirements to specify higher-performance products will increase purchased material and manufacturing costs. The characteristics of required outputs that drive cost are generally identical with the output dictators discussed in the previous section: revenue, derivatives of revenue, outside requirements, structural factors, and requests for service.

Procedures and processes, the way the work is done, is the second general class of cost drivers. Another way of saying this is that costs are driven by the choice of activities and inputs. In general, the two biggest factors that affect procedure and process cost drivers are the degree of automation and the number of things an organization does versus what it buys.

The general *price level* is also a determinant of costs, and this includes the price levels for everything an organization buys: purchased material prices, wage levels, rent levels, and so on. This type of cost driver is usually beyond the manager's control, and price changes can invalidate a budget quickly. (Price levels of important items are always candidates for budget assumptions.)

SUMMARY AND PROCESS: DEFINING THE WORK

For an existing unit, the process of capturing the way things are currently done is neither more nor less than thorough observation and recording. When an existing unit is presented with requirements for new outputs, the process of defining the work is one of design rather than observation: Given a new output, what work (activities) will we do to accomplish it, and what inputs do we need? A new unit must define the work from scratch, and that is the manager's first task.

For all cases, use the following step-by-step process:

1. *Start with the required outputs.*
   - Primary outputs.
   - Their specifications.
   - Information outputs.
   - Service outputs.

Use the general categories of output dictators as a checklist to ensure that nothing has been missed.

2. *Determine what dictates each required output.*
   - Revenue.
   - Derivatives of revenue.
   - Outside requirements.
   - Structural factors.
   - Requests for service.

This both helps you understand the output requirements better and tells you where to look for the amounts and values of outputs that have to be reflected in your budget.

3. *Decide the way you want to do the work to produce the outputs.*

- Define all the tasks involved in producing the outputs.
- Group your conclusions into significant and manageable activities.

4. *Identify the inputs needed for each of the defined activities.*
   - What are the materials (physical or informational) that must be operated on or transformed to achieve this output?
   - What tools, assistance, and support are needed to do this?
   - What instructions are needed?

5. *Iterate among outputs, inputs, and activities to determine the most practical and cost-effective way to produce the outputs.* Inputs needed for preferred activities may be unavailable or too expensive, requiring activities to be changed. Ask the following questions:
   - Is there a better way to do the work?
   - Are there other activities and inputs that will give better performance and/or lower costs in producing the outputs?
   - Since your unit's outputs are another unit's inputs, are there different outputs that will improve overall company performance or reduce company costs?

6. *Determine the causes or drivers of unit costs.*

Concentrate on those things that most strongly determine the organization's cost level. If monthly reports are an incidental cost, don't worry about what drives their costs. In identifying cost drivers, progress from the definition of activities to the nature of the costs to the drivers of those costs. That is, rather than starting with some general categories of cost drivers, look for what drives the individual cost elements: labor, purchased material, rent, utilities, and so forth.

ILLUSTRATION: A PAYROLL UNIT

Most units have more outputs, inputs, and activities than are recognized intuitively, and all are important for a full understanding of the work. Let's use a payroll unit as an example, because all types of businesses have this function. Most people think the work of a payroll unit is conceptually simpler than some functions, so you may be surprised at how many elements its work definition contains (and a particular payroll unit may have more than this example):

Outputs: timely paychecks for every employee, in the right amount, with the correct deductions withheld; all the correct records needed for business, tax, and employee purposes; submission of all required payroll tax returns; and satisfaction of inquiries and complaints.

Inputs: pay and deduction instructions, charging instructions, time records, computer programs, data entry procedures, and general company policies and procedures.

Activities: specifying paycheck and pay stub information (we assume paychecks are actually prepared by data processing, a different unit), reviewing and entering time records, reviewing payroll data prepared by the computer, entering changes in salaries and deductions, correcting errors, making adjustments, delivering paychecks, preparing tax returns, handling inquiries, and administration.

Principal output dictators: number of employees, frequency of paychecks, complexity of pay methods and benefits (for example, overtime, piece work, commissions, numbers and choices of employee medical insurance plans), and the number of states and countries in which served employees work (which determines the number of different income tax withholding schemes that must be accommodated).

Principal cost drivers: all the output dictators, the number of errors and adjustments that must be made, degree of automation of time records, and whether an outside payroll processing service is used.

CHAPTER 7

PLANNING THE UNIT'S WORK

The budget is most fundamentally a plan. More rigorously, it is the numerical expression of a number of related unit plans that add up to the company plan for next year.

After defining the unit's work, the next step is to plan next year's work.

Everyone plans, all the time. Assume you want to go from New York to Chicago. You would not just go out your front door without any thought. The first part of your plan would be to decide whether you want to go by plane, car, train, or bus. The answer may be quick and obvious to you, or the decision may require some work: collecting information on schedules, costs, comfort, and the like.

Assuming you decide to go by car, you still would not just get into your car without further thought. You would first decide what route to take. You would decide whether to drive straight through or stop overnight on the way. In the latter case you would decide where to stop, or you may decide to make that decision when the time comes. You would decide how much money and what supplies to take with you. You would decide whether to have the car serviced.

You would probably not write all this down, at least not in the fancy report or presentation of a typical business plan. However, you would have decided how you were going to get to Chicago before you started the trip.

Planning is just that simple and, at the same time, just that complex. A plan must tell us how we are going to get there from here, after defining what "there" is.

THE ELEMENTS OF BUSINESS PLANNING

A business plan is the determination of the way resources will be used to achieve particular results. To do this, a plan must contain the following elements:

The *goal*—a statement of the desired results to which the plan is addressed. The goal will change as the planning progresses. In the above simple example, the goal of the first planning stage was to decide the best way to go to Chicago. That decision led to another plan whose goal was to determine the best way to go to Chicago by car.

The *"what"*—everything that must be done to achieve the desired results. In the Chicago car trip this includes choosing the route and deciding whether to stop overnight. "Choosing the route" implies an earlier activity of "getting a map." The decision of whether to stop overnight is a prerequisite to the decision of what clothes to take.

The *"how"*—the methods and approaches that will be used to accomplish all the things that must be done. In deciding how to go to Chicago, you might gather timetables and call airlines and railroads yourself, or you might give the whole task to a travel agent. For the car trip itself, the "how" would include the number of drivers and whether to take food or stop for meals.

The *"when"*—the schedule for accomplishing all the activities and the final results. For the Chicago trip, you would start with the date and time you need to be there, working back to when the various decisions must be made. Finally, with the entire plan in hand, the departure date and time would be decided.

The *"how much"*—the resources required to carry out the plan: people, money, particular skills, outside purchased items, etc. Even for the simple example of the Chicago trip, you want to know the total cost, and particular things to buy, like clothes and food.

The above items are the essential elements of any business plan. There are also supporting elements that most plans should contain. These allow justification, evaluation, and proper modification of plans and resulting work:

- The *"why"*—defense of the activities and schedules chosen to achieve the desired results.
- The *assumptions* made in the plan.
- *Contingency plans*, which will be used if assumptions prove incorrect, or particular activities are unsuccessful.
- *Milestones*—the dates and content of important interim results, which allow evaluation of progress relative to the plan.

THE PLANNING WORK OF BUDGETING

If you are new in your job, for your first budget use this year's numbers, unless there is evident reason for change. This should be acceptable; nobody expects you to be an expert budgeter the first time.

This discussion of the general world of planning provides a context for the planning work of budgeting:

The Elements of Budget Planning

Goal	To predict organization outputs, costs, and needs from other organizations
"What" and "how"	The outputs, inputs, and activities that define the organization's work for next year
"When" and milestones	Schedules of outputs, inputs, and activities
"How much"	Costs and needs from other organizations
"Why"	Justification that results in budget approval (See Chapter 11)
Assumptions	Explicit budgeting assumptions
Contingency plans	Generally implicit—part of getting the budget approved

In budgeting, the overall period for the plan is given: the next year. Reduced to essentials, the budgeting process asks each unit manager the question, What outputs can your unit achieve next year at what cost, what particular resources are required, and what do you need from other units and functions? That is the planning *goal* for unit budgeting.

The "what" and the "how" of the budget are the definition of the unit's work for next year. The process for defining the work was laid out in the box entitled "Summary and Process: Defining the Work" (page 52) in Chapter 6. That definition should be done before budgeting begins, because the time pressure makes it difficult to do during budgeting. The task during budgeting, then, is to define that work *for next year*.

In addition to the work definition, the unit manager's starting point is knowledge of this year's costs. Once the manager knows both this year's work definition and costs, the planning focus for many units should be what will change: *How will next year be different from this year?* This focus applies to manufacturing units making roughly the same things from year to year, maintenance service units maintaining the same equipment, payroll and human resources units, and the like.

However, if your unit does different work each year, knowledge of this year's costs and work definition helps only as background knowledge. In an engineering unit that works on design projects, for example, each of those for next year must be defined and planned from scratch in terms of outputs, inputs, and activities.

To plan next year's work in the latter case:

- Start with analysis of the cost drivers to determine which are most important for next year. Knowing this tells the unit manager the most important outputs and activities to focus on, and the combinations of outputs, inputs, and activities whose change will yield the biggest payoffs.

- Identify the type and amount of required outputs. Some outputs will be given to you by bosses and other functions, but most you have to dig out for yourself. The important output dictators you defined usually dictate the places to look for output requirements, such as:

  —Production schedules, for an assembly unit

  —Maintenance schedules, for a customer service unit

  —Operating schedules, for an operations function

  —Customer contracts, for required reports and other compliance activities

  —The legal department, for changes in regulations for handling toxic waste

- Make *assumptions* for those outputs that are unknown, uncertain, and uncontrollable (Chapter 5)

- These specified and assumed outputs determine the amount and type of needed activities, and the resulting needed inputs.

- At first, define the activities only tentatively and then check the availability of inputs, and/or determine if anything has changed about familiar inputs. Then finalize activities and inputs together so they are compatible.

- Inputs may require some temporary assumptions in the early stages of budgeting when available inputs may not be known as yet.

- The unit's costs, determined with the help of the cost drivers, then flow directly from the activities for the given and assumed level of outputs.

- Needs from other organizations flow from the inputs required.

The resulting schedule of all outputs, inputs, and activities is then the "when" of the budget planning. The costs and needs numbers are the "how much." The best ways to generate these numbers are the subjects of Chapters 8 and 9.

All managers define and plan their organization's work to some extent; they could not function otherwise. Doing it deliberately and completely is the best way to prepare good budgets, defend them successfully, react to changes during the budgeting process, and react to problems and surprises throughout the budget year.

ITERATIONS

After your initial budget plan is put together, expect a number of iterations or "reworks" of that plan before it is finalized. The budgets of all the company's units and departments must fit together, and all must be compatible with the company's goals and strategies. Examples of iterations to expect—and, in some cases, to seek—are the following:

- The availability of different kinds of inputs can change the activities, or a better way to do things may be found from a different combination of inputs and activities.
- The amount and kind of required outputs may change as the budget is consolidated and reworked, and as other organizations specify different needs from your unit's.
- The required level of outputs may not be achievable because of resource and capability limitations. Therefore, "resulting outputs" may be different from "required outputs," starting another iteration rippling through the company.

ILLUSTRATIONS

Let's illustrate the preparation of next year's budget plan for both a unit whose work is largely repetitive from year to year and one whose work content changes radically.

The Payroll Unit

For the first, let's again use the same payroll unit that was our example at the end of Chapter 6. You may wish to reread that work definition example (page 54) before proceeding. The payroll unit manager's main concern is to determine what is likely to change next year in terms of required outputs and inputs. Looking first at the cost drivers, a management decision was recently made not to use an outside payroll service. Automation of time records has been discussed but apparently will not be considered for another year at least. Therefore, nothing is expected to change relative to these cost drivers next year. (If the manager is concerned that he or she might be blindsided during the year by a quick decision to change either of these, explicit budgeting assumptions that they will *not* change should be included with the budget.)

In analyzing the cost drivers, the manager finds that the payroll unit workload does not vary much with the number of paychecks, over a wide range, but it does vary with the number of errors and adjustments. These are found to be roughly proportional to the number of employees. The workload also varies significantly with the complexity and number of changes in pay methods and benefits, which have been changing, but not in major ways. Finally, the manager knows of the planned April start-up of a large new facility in a different state, for which the unit will be responsible.

In budgeting, then, the payroll unit manager knows to concentrate on learning planned numbers of employees, changes in pay schemes and benefits, and the tax and compensation regulations of the new state. If numbers of employees are not going to change significantly, and the rate of change of pay schemes and benefits is going to be about the same (again, use assumptions if not confident), this year's work plans and numbers can be used for next year, with one exception: a major planning task is deciding how the work for the new facility will be done. This work must be planned by the manager and the key people from their knowledge and experience and by interacting with people involved with the new facility.

A Machine Shop Unit

As an example of a function whose work is not repetitive, consider a machine shop. Prepared in accordance with Chapter 6, the following is its work definition (in which we separately list the three general types of outputs: primary, information, and service):

Primary outputs:	Machined parts of given types with given specifications
Information outputs:	Reports on use and disposal of toxic materials
	Material requests for raw stock, supplies, and parts
	Budgets
	Monthly reports: output, quality, inventory, costs
Service outputs:	Advice to engineering on design of machined parts
	Incidental machining for management and customers
Output dictators:	Production plan
	Environmental regulations
	Budgeting and reporting requirements
	Incidental requests for machining
Activities:	Prepare material requests
	Receive material
	Maintain inventory
	Set up machines and material
	Machine material
	Inspect output
	Prepare budgets
	Prepare monthly reports
	Store, use, and dispose of toxic material
	Administration
	Other
Inputs:	Raw material
	Supplies
	Drawings and specifications
	Equipment
	Tools

	Training
	Instructions on use of equipment and tools
	Toxic material instructions
	Electricity and other utilities
	Financial numbers
Cost drivers:	All the output dictators
	Type of machinery, and degree of automation
	Work-flow processes
	Location of suppliers
	Price levels for material and supplies

With this analysis in hand, the machine shop manager starts the budgeting with the outputs. The manager needs the actual or assumed production schedule, environmental reporting requirements, and management reporting requirements. From these he or she can forecast the level of activities that will be required next year, and start forecasting the people numbers and skill needs or surpluses, machinery needs, use of electricity and other utilities, and so forth. This leads to conclusions regarding whether the unit can produce the required outputs next year, and what the costs will be.

The most important cost drivers are the production plan, the degree of automation, environmental regulations (because handling toxic material can be expensive), and price levels (for raw materials, electricity, and the like).

Regarding budget assumptions, the first two important cost drivers are not appropriate, because the machine shop manager is expected to contribute to the decisions on the production plan and the degree of automation. However, budget assumptions should be made for environmental regulations (for example, "regulations for the handling of toxic waste will not change significantly during the year") and the most important and volatile prices (for example, "The average cost of machining material will increase 10 percent over this year's prices").

MANAGEMENT PAYOFFS

The budgeting payoff of the work definition and planning is clear, and we have mentioned these things before:

- Understanding the work to be done is the *only* way the budget can be the most probable prediction that is possible.
- It is the best defense of the budget in reviews.
- It facilitates budget changes required in the course of budgeting.
- During the year, it lets you see cause and effect if problems arise in meeting the budget.

Also note the management payoffs beyond budgeting that results from such detailed planning and analysis. In the machine shop example, all the following statements are true management payoffs except one. Which one is false?

- a. Particular output parts requirements may result in abnormal costs and problems. Suggestions for redesign may improve costs and schedules with little or no product performance degradation.
- b. New machinery may increase output or reduce labor costs for a given output, and improve schedules. The analysis plus the cost of the new machinery allows its payoff versus cost to be determined.
- c. The uncertainty about next year has been removed.
- d. By considering individual output requirements (number and schedule) in detail, analysis of activities lets the manager suggest output schedule changes that will improve machine shop efficiency.
- e. For required activities for which the machine shop is not well suited, an intelligent trade-off can be made between subcontracting and acquiring the needed machinery and skills.
- f. The manager now knows what changes will have important effects on the unit, and to what the people

must react. He or she can stay alert for the important changes and not get excited about changes that have minimal effects on the unit.

The false statement is c. You knew that. No matter what we do, next year will be uncertain until it is over.

CHAPTER 8

GENERATING THE BUDGET NUMBERS

Even with good planning for next year, the company still needs numerical predictions of the revenue, costs, and cash flow that will result from all the planned actions.

The numbers that go into next year's budget are necessarily estimates. There is no way you can know exactly what revenues, costs, and other numbers will be next July or August.

THE KINDS OF NUMBERS

Company budgets ultimately predict amounts of:

- Profit
- Revenue
- Cash flow
- Two types of costs:
  —Expense, the day-to-day operating cost that goes into the profit and loss statement (P&L)
  —Capital expenditures, costs of investments—tools, equipment, computers, and the like—that are accumulated separately and charged to the P&L over a series of years.

Company policy and accounting rules determine the costs that are "capitalized" and "expensed."

Unit managers, however, primarily budget costs (and accounting categorizes them into capital or expense). The things that make up their costs are man-hours of effort, all the various purchases needed, number of employees, and the like.

In addition, various unit managers deal with other kinds of numbers, mostly unit outputs, that eventually lead to profit and cash flow, such as:

- Sales managers: orders, revenue
- Manufacturing managers: assemblies, fabrications, tests, shipments, revenue
- Operations managers: transactions of all kinds, hours of operation, service calls, revenue
- Treasury managers: cash receipts

In some companies, unit managers budget these various elements in units of work: man-hours of effort, units assembled and shipped, units purchased, and the like. Accounting then converts these into dollar amounts. In other companies, unit managers do the translation themselves, their submitted budget numbers being dollars. Our discussion will always deal with dollars; estimating work units is always involved and included in that dollar prediction.

Budget assumptions (Chapter 5) are used for all the sources of budget numbers for uncertain and uncontrollable factors, if reliable information is not available.

Additionally, all these kinds of numbers are usually required by product, project, work order number, and the like. Companies want to know the profitability and cash flow of their different products and activities. Therefore, one overall number for revenue, for example, is not enough; revenue by product usually has to be budgeted.

SOURCES OF BUDGET NUMBERS: DATA

To generate all these kinds of budget numbers, the first thing to look for is *data*: values of budget entries substantiated by specific, known information.

- If next year's work plan for a retail store calls for ten hours per day of operation with a given level of service for an anticipated number of customers, the store manager uses data from experience on things like the number of clerks, for example, required to carry out that plan.

- Orders backlog (orders received but not yet sold) to be shipped next year is an example of valid data for a manager who has to predict revenue; these are specific sales that can be predicted with confidence.
- If you are required to predict the costs of 50 units of a given product, and all the material for those products is already in inventory (i.e., bought and paid for), you *know* what the material costs of building those 50 units will be.

Examples of budgeting items for which data can often be used directly in budgeting are:

- Revenue obtained from orders backlog
- Rent
- Salaries of personnel
- Costs of a mature product
- Costs of purchases that have firm quotations
- Costs of doing things that have been done before
- Interest income from fixed investments

Data do not have to be certain to be used directly in the budget. Change the example of having to predict the material costs for building 50 units of a given product to the case in which the material must be bought, rather than just retrieved from inventory. Now you cannot be certain of the material costs. However, if known and trusted vendors say prices will stay the same, you still have valid data: known current prices plus the vendors' statements. You cannot be certain about material costs in this case, but direct data are still the best source of the budget number.

Misuse of Data

When valid and used appropriately, data are the best source of numerical predictions for the budget. The most common misuse is stretching data beyond the time in which they are meaningful. In that same example of predicting material costs for 50 units, now take the case where purchase prices for these materials are unstable and you do not know the vendor. You still have data on current material costs for the product, but those data are not reliable for next year. In this case, a budget assumption must be made for next year's prices, based on the best information and analysis you can find. *In general, current and past data should not be used when uncontrollable outside factors are involved.*

Another example of stretching data is the way that some people labor to put specific customer names and dates on orders expected during next year's fourth quarter. If the order cycle (from initial expression of interest to signing the order) is six months, you cannot possibly know the specific identity of customers who will place orders a year from now. It is better to use trends or equations (perhaps including assumptions) involving such things as market size, known prospects, and number of sales calls.

Being able to fill out your budget forms entirely with data is rare. Many budget numbers are usually generated from either trends or equations.

SOURCES OF BUDGET NUMBERS: TRENDS

If data are not valid for direct use, *trends* are another source. A trend is the rate of change of an item over a period of time. If a particular product had sales of 40, 80, and 120 units, respectively, in the last three years, the trend is an increase of 40 units per year. Applying that trend to budgeting, it predicts that next year's sales will be 160 units.

Learning curves in a factory or any repetitive operation are examples of the use of trends; it is expected that people will complete tasks faster, and thus cheaper, as they become more experienced in doing them.

Seasonal trends are also a source of budget information. Toy and ice cream businesses have obvious seasonal characteristics; many other businesses have seasonal variations just as valid. Since performance against the budget is reviewed and

It is easier for a boss to see that you are not following a trend than to understand that a trend is invalid. Be particularly prepared to justify your conclusion to disregard an established trend.

measured monthly, seasonal characteristics must be correctly reflected.

Precision in trend evaluation is not necessary in budgeting. It is sufficient to estimate a trend by averaging or by plotting the points and visually fitting a straight or curved line to them. If purchase prices for a certain material have increased 4 percent, 7 percent, 6 percent, 3 percent, and 7 percent in each of the last five years, it would be reasonable to say that the trend is a 5–5.5 percent increase per year. Since we are dealing with uncertainty, there is no value in doing the work required to define that trend precisely to a thousandth of a percent.

Always Question Trends

The use of trends to generate budget numbers carries an implicit assumption that the trend will continue. Therein lies the problem. Few trends of any kind last for years; the world changes too fast for conditions that defined the trend to stay the same. More than that, however, the formation of any trend carries no guarantee that it will continue, if changing conditions and uncontrollable factors are at work. Witness the stock market, which often seems to invalidate a trend almost as soon as there is enough data for it to be recognized.

The proper way to use trends in budgeting is always as questioned trends. If the number predicted by the trend is to be used in the budget, a deliberate conclusion must have been reached that the trend will continue. The opposite is also true: To ignore a trend, a deliberate conclusion must have been reached that the trend is no longer valid.

Orders and revenue trends are always suspicious. Cost trends are more reliable, but purchase prices are also uncontrollable, and management actions to change the way things are done invalidate trends. Seasonal trends are also subject to change if certain market characteristics change, or the market puts the products in question to different uses. If the item in question involves uncontrollable outside factors, a budget assumption should be included that either the trend will continue or change.

SOURCES OF BUDGET NUMBERS: EQUATIONS

Budgeting *equations* are algebraic descriptions of the relationship among budget items. They are built with information, knowledge, experience, or assumptions about elements of a total item of interest:

• If you know the cost of doing something once and there are no economies of scale involved, the cost of doing it ten times is simply ten times that unit cost.

• Assume that a sales manager says, "There are 1,000 customers for this product, and they generally replace their equipment every 5 years, so I believe that there will be 200 orders next year." Even if it is never written down, that sales manager has used an equation: next year's orders will equal market size divided by 5.

Budgeting equations must be used when the other sources cannot themselves generate a needed number. The equations are derived from work definition and planning and may use data, trends, and assumptions about both. Equations must also generally be used when budgeting new activities, for which data and trends do not exist. In this case, equations must be developed for outputs and costs from the design and analysis of the new activity. Then data and trends from related activities and general experience must be used in the equations.

Illustration: A Recruiting Unit

Consider a recruiting unit manager whose definition of work has yielded the conclusion that the unit's strongest cost driver is simply the number of positions to be filled, or new hires. This manager can use work planning to structure a simple budgeting equation:

$$\text{Unit cost} = (\text{a fixed amount}) + (\text{cost per new hire}) \times (\text{number of new hires})$$

Data and trends yield a good estimate of the fixed amount and the costs per new hire. There are two sources of required new hires: expansion in the company, and turnover. In such a service organization, the manager must wait for next year's plans for the entire company before the personnel expansion number to use is known. Turnover must be anticipated from data and trends, questioned and analyzed for changing conditions. (This is a prime example of a unit's costs being determined by factors beyond the manager's control, and budget assumptions should be included for division personnel increases and turnover rates.)

Illustration: A Factory Assembly Unit

For a more extensive use of equations, consider a factory assembly unit manager budgeting direct labor costs for next year. The number of units of different products required is obtained from the production schedule (which is the output dictator in this case—if not available, it must be assumed). From knowledge, experience, and work planning, the manager has data on:

- The number of operations required to assemble each product and the time required for each. (These items may be predicted from the data or from the learning curve trend, whichever is appropriate.)
- The wages of the assemblers. (Next year's wage raises may be a budgeting instruction from human resources, or predicted by the manager from known current wages and the trend of previous year's wage raises.)

The direct labor costs per unit per product are then the product of time required for each and the wage costs per unit of time. That is,

Labor cost per unit = (assembly time in hours)
$$\times \text{ (wage cost per hour)}$$

Then

$$\text{Labor cost per product} = (\text{labor cost per unit}) \times (\text{number of units})$$

and

$$\text{Total labor costs} = \text{the sum of the labor costs for each product}$$

The manager's task that surrounds these computations is to plan and lay out the work in the most effective and efficient manner, minimizing the idle time and maximizing output versus cost. This planning should be done before the computations and redone afterward, to see if the numbers point the way to improvements in the work plan. For a new product, the manager uses the same equations but must design the process to be used and apply operation timing data from similar products and experience.

Misuse of Equations

Misuse of equations in budgeting can be caused by using the wrong equations, of course—by not properly relating cause and effect. Truly understanding the drivers and dictators of outputs and costs through work definition and planning is the best antidote. There is no substitute for unit managers understanding their units' work. The other most prominent misuse is not using equations enough, that is, using direct data and trends beyond the time for which they are valid.

SUMMARY

There are three sources of numerical predictions in the budget: data, trends, and equations.

- *Data* should always be used when available and valid for the particular application.
- *Trends* should never be ignored, but they should always be questioned before use. If uncontrollable fac-

Stretching data, using invalid trends, taking more time, or striving for great precision won't take the uncertainty out of the future.

tors are involved, such trends should be treated with assumptions.

• *Equations* are used when the other sources cannot themselves generate a needed number. They also must be used when budgeting new activities for which data and trends do not exist.

OTHER POINTS ON NUMBER GENERATION

Some important points about budget number generation were made in Chapter 3 when you were getting your feet wet in filling out a budget form. To refresh your memory, these points are repeated here.

• Remember that precision is not accuracy. If all you can really predict about telephone costs next year is that they will be between $2,000 and $2,500, there is no value in putting $2,378 in the budget. In fact, it is harmful, because the four figures mislead by implying more knowledge than you have. In such a case, please put $2,400 in your budget.

• Use perspective on budget line item entries. Major costs require extensive, intelligent analysis, because the impact of a mistake is large. If a particular line item is only 2 percent of your total budget, however, don't waste time on it. Even if you are wrong by half, it only causes a 1 percent error in your total budget. Future uncertainty does not allow your whole budget to be that accurate.

• To implement that perspective, categorize outputs and costs into major, minor, or in between (which we called "substantial").

- If *minor*, spend minimum time on them, possibly just using this year's number or a quick guess at next year's amount.
- If *substantial*, it depends on whether the unit's work is largely repetitive from year to year or changes radically (as illustrated in Chapter 7 regarding work planning). If next year's work will be:
  —*Similar* to this year's, plan and analyze next year's work for changes and use those to modify this year's data
  —*Different* from this year's, use work plans and appropriate analyses of data, trends, and equations to get the predicted numbers
- If *major*, do the best and most extensive analysis of work plans and different number sources, because the penalty for a bad prediction is large.

APPLICATION

Since *costs* constitute the great majority of budget number generation, Chapter 9 is devoted to budgeting costs.

Revenue budgeting varies greatly across different kinds of businesses:

- Many retail businesses, for example, are *cash businesses in which revenue is made up of many small sales*. Data on individual customers are meaningless. Data or trends on past and current month-by-month sales (revenue) may be useful, but their applicability must be questioned. (For example, the opening or closing of a large factory nearby is a new condition that changes the sales trend for many retail businesses.) Revenue is often predicted from equations or statistical models of the served market.

• *Businesses that respond to orders* have a different revenue budgeting problem. An order is an agreement to buy something at a specified future time and price, and often implies that work must be done before delivery (for example, construction projects, military systems). For such businesses, backlog (orders received but not yet delivered) is confident data that can be used directly. Orders prospects are budgeting data if confidence in an eventual order is high. Beyond identified prospects, trends and equations (or market models) are usually the best sources.

• *Businesses that rely on a few large orders* (such as airplane or supercomputer manufacturers) have a particularly difficult time budgeting revenue, because single orders are so important. Trends and statistical models are no help, because so few prospects are involved. Data from backlog and confident orders prospects are useful in budgeting. Otherwise, budgeted revenue must come from analysis of a relatively small number of individual customers.

Beyond costs and revenue, other budget numbers that have to be generated are primarily *unit outputs*: shipments, assemblies, transactions, service calls, and so on. If such outputs are directly customer driven (like bank loan closings or some kinds of customer service calls), they are predicted like revenue. If they are internally driven (like assemblies or shipments), numbers come from the work plans and all three number sources, as appropriate. For example:

- Shipments or cash receipts would be entered as data from production and revenue/collection plans.
- Numbers of assemblies could be obtained from learning curve trends.
- Assemblies could be obtained from equations involving number of assemblers, assembly operations, and time per operation.

CHAPTER 9

BUDGETING COSTS

Remember that acceptance of a product or service by a customer is a result; everything else is a cost. Management is paid to get results and minimize costs, all costs.

With the work definition and plans in hand, what do you have to know to budget costs? You have to:

- Understand the nature of the costs the unit will incur.
- Understand relationships that may exist among certain costs.
- Know how to estimate individual item costs (which then have to be summed into aggregate cost predictions for next year).
- Be able to insert predicted costs into the budget with the proper timing.

These are all covered in this chapter.

THE NATURE OF BUSINESS COSTS

A straightforward way to categorize business costs is into things that the company makes or does (*personnel costs*), and things that the company buys (*purchase costs*).

Personnel Costs

Personnel costs are labor and employee benefits. Labor costs are salaries, wages, commissions, bonuses, and such things as overtime premiums, if applicable. Benefits are vacation and holiday pay, sick pay, insurance, and the like. Conventionally, if outside contractors are used to accomplish work, rather than employees, that is a purchase cost.

Personnel costs are conceptually simple, but their accounting treatment, and therefore their budgeting, ranges from simple to quite complex. (See the Glossary for definitions of accounting terms used in budgeting.) For example:

- In some retail businesses and many small businesses, labor costs are simply the salaries and benefits of the employees.
- Manufacturing businesses generally wish to keep track of their direct expense, to know the profitability of their various products. To do that, time spent on (charged to) direct labor on each project or product must be known, and time records are kept of how employees spend and charge their time. Employees are often labeled as direct or indirect. The indirect people—all general and administrative people, managers, engineers, planners, secretaries—ordinarily charge their time to indirect labor.

Every industry, and every company to some extent, groups and accounts for both personnel and purchase costs differently. Rather than dwelling on generalities here, you must learn the specifics of how your company does it, and the terms that are used. The accounting people and your boss are the best sources of this information.

Purchase Costs

Purchase costs include:

- Things directly related to revenue, such as inventory for a retail or distribution business, and raw materials and components for a manufacturing business
- Investments (called capital expenditures) necessary to produce revenue or generally to conduct business, including factory and store equipment, buildings or improvements to leased facilities, tools, computers, and trucks
- Personnel-related costs, such as memberships, subscriptions, travel and living, and training

Be alert for those old favorites of managements everywhere: arbitrary freezes on head count or overtime. If the work to be done is not reduced, these will not reduce costs.

- Facilities-related costs, such as rent, utilities, maintenance and repair, and security guards
- Outside services, such as consultants, legal expense, design and drafting services, and temporary personnel
- Other: advertising and sales promotion, taxes, board of directors costs, freight, contributions, and the like.

With these general categories and examples as guides, you must learn your unit's specific cost elements. *Get help from accounting to ensure that you are aware of all types of costs your organization incurs.* Accountants are trained to recognize all the types of cost involved in an endeavor, as well as being the best source for how the different costs are grouped and treated.

COST RELATIONSHIPS

Every unit has costs that are related to other costs. Budgeters must understand these relationships so they don't kid themselves about what their real costs will be.

In some cases, a first cost automatically gives rise to a second kind of cost. For example, the cost of high-priced professional people necessarily includes costs of things that keep them current in their professions, such as memberships, seminars, courses, books, and magazines. If the business needs these professional people, management must accept that such supporting expenses are necessary costs of doing business.

In other cases, some costs unavoidably increase if others are cut. Further, if the current way of doing things is the most efficient way, total costs will increase if one of the cost elements is arbitrarily cut. For example:

- If the amount of work stays the same, employee reductions must be made up by using outside contractors or higher overtime costs.
- If there is a given amount of remote work to be done—selling, customer contact, working with proj-

ect partners, dealing with a department in a distant city, etc.—travel and telecommunications expense cannot both be reduced. If managers cut travel expense, they must expect telecommunications expense to increase.

The only ways to cut costs are to find more efficient ways to do a given amount of work, or to do less work. Managers need to guard against the illusion that cutting one element of cost $X will produce $X overall saving, if the work is not changed.

As usual, the specifics of such relationships are unique for each unit and have to be learned from definition and understanding of the work.

COST ESTIMATING

Prediction of next year's costs must be anchored on the proper use of data, trends, and equations (Chapter 8).

A number of costs are always directly predictable from data. Rent is an example. Costs of most things that have been done before are in this category, such as mature product assembly, restaurant personnel costs, tax return preparation. Things that change slowly, such as office supplies and payroll costs, should be adequately predictable from data. Things that are bought in predictable amounts at established prices become usable data as soon as the price is known: utilities, taxes, audit fees, and so on. Where valid data is in hand, it should always be used.

Trends are valuable for predicting the costs of controllable things, but trends in the pertinent outside environment must be analyzed and questioned. Learning curves of all kinds are examples of the former. The cost of fuel for an airline is an example of the latter; oil prices change quickly, and recent data can be useless as a predictor. Things like that fuel cost are candidates for budget assumptions.

Many companies require salary planning of some sort from all unit managers. Budgeted personnel costs must, of course, be consistent with that salary planning.

Equations come into play when data or trends do not directly yield the item needed, as when predicting costs for new activities and finding new ways to do old activities. When automation is to be substituted for labor, for example, cost equations for the automated approach are the usual and proper way to justify the expenditure involved.

The other "anchor" for next year's cost predictions is to use the best information available. Let's discuss this separately for personnel and purchase costs.

Estimating Personnel Costs

There are two aspects of personnel costs to discuss: the work to be done, and the costs of the employees. The first step is to predict the work to be done in terms of the number of people required, or the man-hours (or man-days) of effort required. The result is often requirements either for hiring new people or for laying off current employees. Then the number of people or the man-hours effort times predicted salaries (or direct labor rates) and benefits equals the personnel cost.

Part of the prediction of the work to be done is easy, part difficult. The effort required to do repetitive tasks that have been done before, in the same way, is easy to predict. There are direct data available.

Doing old tasks in a new way is the first degree of difficulty. The new activities have to be planned, and the new effort required follows directly from that planning.

More difficult is the estimation of the effort required to do new tasks or new projects. Again, the planning and definition of the work to be done (the activities) are the bases for estimating the man-hours effort or the number of people required. If the new task involves new, unfamiliar activities, they must be estimated from knowledge of similar work. If no one has such knowledge and experience, the new activities must be divided into elements to which knowledge and experience can be applied.

Get help from the purchasing professionals to estimate important purchase costs.

Consider a bank installing its first automatic teller machines. With no direct data, how does it budget the personnel costs for servicing and maintaining the machines? Possibly a consultant, or a new employee with experience elsewhere, can supply direct knowledge and experience. Otherwise the planning must break down the service and maintenance into familiar activities, such as counting and stocking currency, preventive maintenance on electronic and electromechanical devices, and monitoring computer transactions.

Estimating Purchase Costs

For things that are bought, the simplest costs to estimate are those bought at *known price and quantity*. Items with price labels, price lists, and catalogs are in this category. Simple, reliable data are available as the basis for next year's cost estimate. Known forthcoming price changes are also simple and reliable data.

POSSIBLE PRICE CHANGES

Expected or possible price changes require judgment, which should be assisted by the best information that can be obtained about future prices. If there is a good relationship with known vendors, they are the best source of information about their future prices. Otherwise, trends should be used, but only after analysis for changes in their causes. Electricity rates may have gone up, or down, for years, but that trend can change suddenly if the industry, market, or financial environment has changed for the electric utility. All available information should be used in estimating such a cost for next year; if the cost is important, uncertain, and uncontrollable, an assumption should be made.

Next to catalog items in simplicity to predict are things for which *firm quotations* are in hand. Firm quotations from suppliers are the only fully accurate way to cost the things bought for new products or activities. Firm quotations are data, and should be used as such.

Sometimes firm quotations cannot be obtained, and the best information available is a *vendor estimate*, sometimes called a "budgetary quotation." In most situations, this estimate is the best data available, and the manager's cost estimate should be based on it. However, again, judgment must be applied, because that estimate does not represent a binding commitment on the part of the vendor. As usual, all sources of information should be used: vendor past reliability, analyzed trends, estimates from multiple vendors, industry intelligence, and so forth.

Finally, there are *known things whose quantity and price will vary*, such as future utility rates, food for a restaurant, and various commodities. Such predictions are always judgments, and the experience of the right operating and purchasing people is often the best guide for these judgments. If important, these are always candidates for budget assumptions.

Accounting may move or change the budgeted costs you submit. That is not a problem as *your boss* and *accounting* understand the reality of how the work will be done and how the costs will actually be incurred.

THE TIMING OF BUDGETED COSTS

Accountants often spread costs, to give a better continuing picture of the health of the business. A large one-time cost, for example, may be spread on the profit and loss statement (P&L) so that one twelfth of that cost appears in each month. Or a monthly average estimate may be accrued for something like legal costs, to be adjusted later in the year if actual costs differ from the estimate.

Budgeters, on the other hand, should *accurately reflect timing* of costs. If you have a large one-time cost, reflect it in the budget in the month you expect it to be incurred. Also, say a particular cost is $3X per quarter, but it is invoiced quarterly, not monthly. Do not average that cost $X per month; budget it as $3X four times a year, in the months that the invoice is received.

The reason is that you will be monitored and measured monthly, or at least quarterly, on your budgeted costs. Let the accountants spread and average if they like, but ensure that you present your best prediction of reality, so no one will get too excited if a given month is either well above or below the averaged budget.

On the other hand, for relatively unimportant costs that vary from month to month, *averaging* in your budget submission may be appropriate. Just make sure that everyone knows your submission is an expected average.

One of the usual rules of accrual accounting for unusual and major expenses is to *charge an anticipated cost* to the P&L as soon as it is known. Severance costs are accrued when the layoff decision is made, not when salary continuation is paid. Large purchases are charged when the purchase commitment is made, not when the invoice is received or paid. For the timing of budget entries for such major or unusual cost items, make sure that you put costs in the month that the accountants will enter (charge) them. Consult accounting for guidance.

Accountants also add *cost reserves* to budgeted and actual numbers. They might reserve (anticipate) the costs of the settlement of a lawsuit, for example. A reserve more likely to affect unit budgets is an inventory obsolescence reserve— if you are responsible for some inventory, you may be charged a monthly expense to reflect the decrease in value of that inventory with age. Such a reserve charge has to be done consistently within generally accepted accounting principles, and so is the province of the accountants. Managers have nothing to do, except to find out and understand what the accountants are doing to their budgets, and to again ensure that their bosses understand it.

Unit managers may, however, become involved with cost reserves, and sometimes should. Say that a manager recognizes the possibility, but not the certainty, of a large and unusual repair expense in next year's third quarter. Depending on the circumstances and the company's practices, the manager possibly should suggest accruing costs against that contingency during each month of next year. This is financial recognition of a possible problem, which is sometimes appropriate.

Seasonal trends must be reflected correctly in budget entries. Consider the credit department of a large appliance dealer who offers extended payment terms at Christmas. A peak of collection activity will then come in February and March, requiring higher expenses for such things as overtime, telephone expense, computer time, and perhaps temporary personnel. Most organizations have some sort of variation of activity, and thus costs, across the year. No manager wants to have to explain an apparent over-budget situation that is simply the result of averaging out such seasonal variations.

The guiding principle regarding timing of budget entries is that higher management wants to understand the health and progress of the company at all times, not just the end of the year. Therefore, managers' performance versus budget will be monitored and measured monthly or quarterly. It is not enough to make good estimates of total annual costs; the estimates must also be good for each quarter and month. The accountants may blur the monthly picture for good reason with their treatments; but they and your boss must understand the underlying reality of when costs will be incurred.

CHAPTER 10

PUTTING IT ALL TOGETHER

Let's briefly review what has been said about the budget and the unit manager's work of budgeting:

- Company budgets are the financial expression of company plans for next year. They are the sum of all the budgets of company component organizations, suitably transformed by accounting into higher management and financial reporting terms.
- Unit budgets are not done, or approved, in a vacuum. They must reflect company strategies and plans, management priorities, and the needs and desires of interfacing organizations. Outputs to, and needs from, other organizations are defined in the process of planning the work and given value when generating the numbers.
- The planning work of budgeting:
  —Its goal is to define, for next year, the organization's outputs (which are usually inputs to other organizations), costs, and needs (inputs) from other organizations.
  —The timing and schedules of all these must be included.
  —The proper way to define the work is in terms of outputs, activities, and inputs, together with the things that dictate the outputs and drive the costs.
  —Next year's outputs and inputs are never fully known at budget time. The planning must reflect that uncertainty with estimates from the best information available and explicit assumptions for those things that are uncontrollable.

- Generating the budget numbers:
    —Unit budgeters primarily predict costs, but some also budget revenue and various kinds of outputs.
    —The budget numbers flow directly from the unit work plan: the outputs, costs, needs from other organizations, and schedules.
    —The sources of budget numbers in all prediction areas are data, trends, and equations.
    —Explicit assumptions should supply the numbers for uncontrollable items for which none of the sources is available.
    —Personnel costs are predicted from work plans and wage and salary information. If possible, purchase costs are predicted from published prices and firm quotations. When that is impossible, the best data, trends, and knowledge must be used.

The key to getting all this budgeting work done is to *recognize the severe time pressure* inherent in most company budgeting processes. Once budgeting begins, budgeters can be overwhelmed by urgent information gathering and number crunching. Things like planning the work and learning company practices must be completed before that happens.

Therefore, before we get to the final element of budgeting work ("Getting the Right Budget Approved"—Chapter 11), we need to discuss how to organize budget preparation efficiently. We will discuss the unit budgeter's process in terms of:

- Work that should be done before company budgeting begins ("preparatory work")
- Work done during the company budgeting process ("budget generation")

A useful intermediate step, a preliminary budget, should also be included in the budgeter's process, and will be discussed.

If this pre-liminary work seems heavy, take consolation in the fact that every item will help you manage better, and all these prepara-tory tasks are major efforts only the first time they are done.

PREPARATORY WORK

To develop good budgets, unit managers should do the following before the company's budgeting process begins:

• Learn the company's budgeting process, forms, ter-minology, and relevant accounting usage. The best sources are accounting and your boss.

• Learn everything you can about your boss's priorities, company and division strategies and plans, accounting's priorities and points of emphasis, and the business environ-ment and financial constraints in which the company expects to operate next year. This will never be found on one piece of paper, but must result from extensive reading and contin-uing discussions with bosses, accounting people, and mar-keting people.

• Define the organization's current work and known forthcoming changes, in terms of outputs, inputs, activities, output dictators, and cost drivers.

• Program your budget forms onto a spreadsheet pro-gram in your personal computer, for later ease of manipula-tion and modification.

The scheduling of this work depends on the situation. The important thing is to have it all completed when the com-pany's budgeting process begins. If being done for the first time, start at least a couple of months before budgeting begins, given that this has to be a part-time activity.

THE PRELIMINARY BUDGET

A practice that unit managers will find quite useful is the preparation of a preliminary budget as soon as possible after budgeting begins, that is, *as soon as any requirement information and instructions are received.*

What exactly does a preliminary budget mean in the sense used here? It means a broad prediction of next year's outputs and costs, accurate to within 10 to 15 percent of the final

If budget forms have been programmed into your personal computer, the mechanics of generating preliminary budgets, plus analysis of alternatives, is easy.

budget. As opposed to the bottom-up numerical construction of the final budget, it is a top-down prediction based on experience, equations, and trends, without detailed analysis of all the different costs.

Some managers are uncomfortable making the approximations and broad estimates that such a preliminary budget requires. They want to know "everything" before putting pencil to paper. However, they must understand that (1) they cannot know "everything" during budget time, (2) they are smart enough to make broad estimates that are good enough for the purpose, and (3) the benefits of such a quick estimate outweigh the discomforts.

How to Do It

The idea is to make a quick prediction to see if the unit's plans are in the ballpark before doing all the number crunching. If your plans are way off (for example, not even close to accomplishing the required outputs, or apparently require a cost increase when a cost reduction has been dictated), time spent on detailed cost and output prediction would be wasted; your budget would be disapproved and all that work would have to be redone.

To do a preliminary budget, fill in all items on the budget form, but do it as follows:

- Use the output requirements and instructions that you have been given.
- Make the most informed guess you can about needed information not yet received.
- Predict achievable outputs and costs from experience and equations without doing detailed analysis.

The best way to do that last item depends on the nature of the unit's work and function:

- If the unit experiences little year-to-year variability (such as a payroll function in stable times), just use this year's actuals, plus a quick estimate of the effects of any known coming changes.

- For a function whose outputs and work change greatly from year to year (such as factory assembly), its basis has to be work definition and plans. Compare and contrast next year's requirements with this year and last year. Predict the budget numbers from experience where comparable, make an informed guess at work elements that are not comparable, and particularly highlight the latter for further analysis.
- Between these two extremes (units like purchasing or branch bank operations), a combination of this year's actuals plus a few equations can be used.

As an example of the latter, a purchasing manager may conclude, in defining the organization's work, that there is a steady level of activity plus a variable component that depends on the number of new products manufactured during a year. The relationship for the variable component may be something like

$$\text{Variable man-hours} = \text{constant} \times \text{number of new products}$$

This manager's preliminary budget would then be current year actual costs plus or minus amounts arising from the difference between the number of new products in the current year versus the next (budget) year.

Benefits

The first benefit of this preliminary budget was already noted above: You get early warning, before doing a lot of number crunching, of plans that lead to budgets that are going to be disapproved.

Other benefits are as follows:

- It quickly highlights budgeting problems, such as mismatches of resources and requirements, and allows budgeters to focus on such problems as budgeting proceeds.

- It indicates the information needed to complete the budget. Budgeters can then immediately concentrate on obtaining the missing information, rather than having to spend time in defining and understanding what is missing.
- It illuminates important areas for next year, those in which performance improvements and cost reductions will have large payoffs.
- It lets budgeters immediately begin informed communications with bosses and peers to resolve budgeting problems and "sell" their approach to the budget and their problem solutions.

BUDGET GENERATION

If the preparatory work and the preliminary budget have been done well, budget generation will not be the onerous, time-consuming task that it usually is.

Most of the work during budget generation is predicting all the cost, revenue, and output numbers required. Initial concentration should be on:

- Obtaining missing information regarding required outputs and inputs
- Communicating with interfacing organizations concerning needs and desires back and forth
- Finalizing budget assumptions, when needed information on required outputs and inputs becomes available
- Communicating with the boss, accounting, and interfacing organizations every step of the way

The communication steps are extremely important. That the budget cannot be done in a vacuum bears repeating. For the company to succeed, all organization budgets must be consistent and complementary. The budget is worthless if top management strategy calls for equal emphasis on widgets and gadgets, sales budgets orders for 10,000 widgets and only 100 gadgets, and manufacturing plans to build 8,000 gadgets and 2,000 widgets. Most inconsistencies are not that obvious, but they do not have to be to have bad effects on company success.

To discuss the actual generation of the budget numbers, it is appropriate to summarize this chapter briefly. The best way to generate the budget numbers is as follows:

- Before budgeting begins, define the unit's work and understand the important equations, output dictators, and cost drivers involved.
- As budgeting begins, use that information and data on current operations to prepare a preliminary budget, based on early information about next year's required outputs and available inputs.
- Then, as work is done and information is developed, appropriately use data, questioned trends, equations, assumptions, knowledge, and experience to generate the numbers that will be submitted, as discussed in Chapters 8 and 9.

This process uses data where possible, trends where valid, and equations and assumptions for the rest of the predictions. It uses all pertinent information about the company, the organization, and next year as soon as it becomes available. The result will be a budget with the best possible prediction of next year's numbers, given the inherent uncertainty and uncontrollability of the future.

CHAPTER 11

GETTING THE RIGHT BUDGET APPROVED

The final task of budgeting is *selling* the budget; a good budget means nothing unless it is approved. While expressed as numbers of dollars, budget approval really means the acceptance and authorization of your plans for next year, including:

- Expected and committed results
- Resources required to achieve the results
- Work plans, including improvement programs and cost reductions
- Support (inputs) required from other organizations.

In other words, *budget approval equals approval of the definition of the job to be done next year, and of the resources required to do that job.*

Getting the right budget approved is not a trivial task. It requires the same level of energy and focus that must be applied to the rest of the work of budgeting. We can identify three aspects of the budget approval task: objective, environmental, and psychological:

1. *Objective* means the independent reality and logic of the submitted budget relative to the job to be done.
2. *Environmental* refers to situational factors outside the budget itself, such as company financial health, that affect the approval of a given budget.
3. *Psychological* refers to the subjective factors involved.

Sadly, many people do not realize the importance of credibility until they have ruined it by *not* delivering as forecast too many times. Then they wonder why they have trouble getting the boss to approve their proposals and budgets.

While distinct, these three aspects of obtaining budget approval are closely related, and overlap in some cases. The dictates of all three must be observed; they are roughly equal in importance.

OBJECTIVE ASPECTS OF SELLING THE BUDGET

Not surprisingly, the first requirements of the objective aspects of getting budget approval are to have *justifications for all numbers and forceful arguments for all proposed courses of action*. The first step in satisfying this requirement is to give the budget a logical basis by planning the work and generating the numbers as explained in this book.

In such a firm grounding, assumptions are particularly important and useful in the approval process. Managers should always be willing to change assumption values if their bosses so wish; the key point is to get the boss's agreement that that item in question *is* an appropriate assumption, i.e., uncontrollable by the manager and therefore something on which the manager should not be measured.

Additionally, there are *personal characteristics* that facilitate the objective aspects of budget approval.

Credibility

It is difficult to overemphasize the importance of a person's building a reputation for doing what he or she has promised. Many business plans and proposals are difficult to evaluate objectively; the planner/proposer often knows more about the subject than the reviewers. This is generally true of budgets—if you say you need ten people to do something new, the boss seldom has firm data and knowledge to dispute your estimates. Your past record in being right and accomplishing things as promised can thus carry heavier weight than anything else in the boss's evaluation.

Good Presentation

The presentation should be accurate, clear, well supported, and to the point. Always keep in mind that the purpose of budget presentations is to *sell*. Neither assume it will be accepted without supporting arguments nor drown the listener in extraneous data.

Numerical and typographical errors on presentation aids are interesting examples of credibility at work. Most bosses will accept one or two such errors without effect. Have a few more such errors and the boss will conclude you are sloppy. However, too many (and each boss has his or her own threshold) will make the boss conclude that you do not know what you are talking about. Are not such easily corrected errors a silly way to lose credibility with the boss?

Good Answers

The final important personal characteristic is having ready and lucid answers to the questions that arise. Here there is no substitute for knowledge of your job and of how the boss and other reviewers react to things. What are their "hot buttons," current problems, and priorities? Every budget submission and presentation should be reviewed beforehand for anticipated questions, and submitters should make sure that they have good answers ready for these.

ENVIRONMENTAL ASPECTS

Assume that top management decides to "run out" a certain line of business, investing no more money in it but working to obtain all cash possible before it ends. Now assume that the crusading sales manager for that business line submits a budget that doubles the sales effort for next year, in the belief that this business can be saved and made to grow again. That sales manager will undoubtedly have his head handed to him at the first budget review. He ignored an important factor when he developed his budget: Top management has decided not to invest for growth.

This is an example of the environmental aspects of budget approval at work. Budgeters must be aware of, and take into account, all the pertinent factors outside their own units. Pertinent environmental factors include at least:

- The financial condition of the company or division
- The state of the relevant outside environments: economy, market, competition, and government regulation
- The current reputation and job security of the boss, and his or her bosses
- Company and division strategy and plans, particularly those regarding growth or de-emphasis of activities in which the given unit is involved.

Cautions

If your unit is part of a department that is on shaky ground, the situation is tricky. If the shakiness is due to loss of credibility of the department head, probably no aggressive initiatives within that department's budgets will be approved. On the other hand, if the shakiness is due to recent poor performance and the work of the department is essential to the company, aggressive initiatives may be most welcome. Top management may be convinced that something different must be done within this department, and therefore is looking for such aggressive initiatives.

The environmental aspects of budget approval that are internal to the company are complex. It is often difficult, sometimes impossible, for unit managers to judge the true internal environment correctly. It is even more difficult for them to predict the effects on budget approval, because they are never privy to all the knowledge and the resulting perspective of top management.

Therefore, there is an important caution pertinent to attempting to factor these internal environmental aspects into budgeting: Do not guess, or assume you know the facts. Estimating company politics is a favorite sport of people everywhere, and the estimates are usually wrong. Get your boss to communicate with you, and act on that communication plus whatever real data, rather than fairy tales, you can learn.

What a Budgeter Must Do

It has now been said that these environmental aspects of budget approval are important, but that managers often cannot know all of the pertinent factors. That unsatisfactory situation is unfortunately the truth. So what should a budgeter do?

- As usual, communicate, communicate, communicate. Listen to what the boss says, and to what higher management says and watch closely what they do. Do not wait until budget submission to check an observation with the boss; do it early in the process so that you will be on the same page with him or her.

- Pay strict attention to the environmental factors that you know are true, such as a bad economy, cancellation of company credit lines, or aggressive behavior by the competition. Reflect those facts clearly in your budget. Any optional aggressive growth initiatives should ordinarily be proposed in good times, not bad times. Cost reductions and productivity improvements should be emphasized in bad times.

- Never let environmental factors overwhelm the objective aspects of your planning. If confident that new equipment will have a good payoff in reduced cost or improved performance, never fail to propose it in the budget because of perceived negative environmental factors. Even if they disapprove because of hard times, you want the bosses to know about your idea.

- Never do illogical budgeting because of perceived environmental factors. If you are convinced that you need more resources next year, never cut costs in the budget just because you believe that is what management wants. Think of the consequences that will result if you are wrong.

- Finally, ignore the gossip about environmental factors that cannot be confirmed. Concentrate only on what is best for your organization, your boss's organization, and interfacing functions. The worst thing that can happen is that you will be sent back to redo the budget. You will not lose points for persuasively pushing what is best for your part of the company, despite a contrary indicator that you could not be expected to know.

THE PSYCHOLOGICAL ASPECTS

While you have just been told that sometimes you should ignore certain environmental factors, never ignore the psychological aspects of budgeting.

Boss versus Budgeter

The psychological nature of budgeting follows unavoidably from:

- The conflict in objectives in which the boss wants the best results possible, and for the unit to be challenged, while the submitting unit budgeter (the subordinate) wants a budget that can be beaten.
- The fact that both boss and subordinate are dealing with uncertainty: Neither knows what the future will hold, or even exactly what resources they will need to do a specified job

With these contradictory objectives plus the uncertainty, both boss and subordinate go through a mental process of estimating the other's state of mind.

Subordinates must begin the thought process with good budget content, so that they know the allowable limits of the forthcoming negotiation with their bosses. After that, the first question is, How will the boss react to these numbers? Budgeters should think about the boss's attitude generally, reaction to past budgets, what he or she has said or done lately, and current pressures. Budgeters should also judge how smart the boss is, where he or she can be fooled, and where the subordinate had better not try to fool him or her. The distillation of all such thinking determines the transition from what the budgeter thinks is a realistic budget to the "padded" budget that actually should be submitted.

Bosses also get a turn, of course, and they have the advantage because they are in the controlling position and are reacting rather than initiating. Bosses consider whether the subordinates are optimists or pessimists, their record in meeting commitments, whether they are polished game players, their knowledge of the situation, and general intelligence. The boss usually has a preconceived idea of approximately what the subordinate's budget should be, and this is ordinarily modified somewhat by good subordinate input.

Boss and subordinate eventually arrive at an agreed budget, with which each has varying degrees of comfort. (As in any negotiation, the result is probably better if both sides have roughly an equal degree of discomfort.)

How to Play the Game

How should the budgeter, armed with good plans for next year's work and good budget numbers, play this psychological game? It depends on the nature of the budgeter's boss, and the relationship between budgeter and boss.

The best situation is the one that allows the budgeter to be straightforward and objective. If the boss is competent and reasonable and the relationship is good, this is the recommended approach. The subordinate's cost estimates, after all, are intellectually grounded, not emotional. The best budget will result if the arguments are about specific outputs, activities, inputs, or assumptions. These are the arguments that bosses and subordinates are supposed to have, and they and the company will be better off if these are the arguments joined in budget negotiations.

On the other hand, if the conditions of a good relationship with a good boss are not present, budgeters must protect themselves. They should still base their arguments on the planning and definition of their work, and associated assumptions. However, it is difficult to overcome emotion with logic. If subordinates believe their budgets will be subject to emotional attack (and if they do not know, this is the safest assumption to make), they should "pad" their budgets dis-

Take budgeting seriously. Better budgeting can increase your job satisfaction, make you better able to cope with the problems that will undoubtedly come next year, and enhance your career.

creetly and cleverly as a defense against emotion and arbitrary cuts.

Such padding is the enemy of good budgeting, but *the budgeter's first responsibility is to get approval of the resources needed to do next year's required work.* It is seldom as simple as adding 5 percent to everything because the boss is known to make 5 percent arbitrary cuts. It usually takes all the intelligence and perception that the budgeter can bring to bear.

SELLING YOUR BUDGET

In short, the best basis for getting your budget approved is concentrated attention on the following:

- Proper intellectual grounding of the budget in the organization work plan, and the use of the best sources for budget numbers
- A good reputation and good presentations
- Appropriate attention to environmental factors
- Skilled playing of the psychological games
- Close and continual communication with the boss

The obvious, gross basis for the last requirement is that one of the worst things you can do is surprise the boss unpleasantly at budget time. That is almost guaranteed to make the budget negotiation emotional. However, a basis that is just as important is that the boss will understand your budget, because the boss was privy to your reasoning as it developed. And you will understand the boss's state of mind, and the degree of approval or disapproval of various items, before budget reviews begin.

Here is one last question. True or false: Implementation of these directives guarantees budget approval.

Unfortunately, the correct answer is "false." The psychological world of budgeting can be full of surprises, and the pertinent environmental factors can never be fully known. Still, the recommended process for selling your budget will give you the best possible chance for approval and also put you in the best possible position to react to any surprises that the budget approval process brings.

GLOSSARY: ACCOUNTING TERMS USED IN BUDGETING

accounts payable   Amounts owed by a business for purchases received and accepted.

accounts receivable   Amounts owed to a business by customers for goods and services received and accepted.

accrual accounting   An accounting basis in which revenue is recorded when earned and costs and balance sheet changes are recorded when commitments are made. Large, one-time expenses can also be averaged over the year or a portion thereof.

accrued expense   A cost recorded as expense that represents future actual expenditure.

accumulated depreciation   The total depreciation of a fixed asset from its purchase to the present time.

allocated cost   Cost of one type that is assigned or charged to costs of other types.

amortization   Prorating the cost of an asset, liability, or expenditure over a specified period of time.

asset   Anything owned that has monetary value.

backlog   Orders that have been received but not yet delivered. Also called sales backlog or orders backlog.

balance sheet   A financial statement showing the assets, liabilities, and equity of a business as of a certain date.

book value   The current accounting worth of a business or a balance sheet item. For a fixed asset, it equals cost minus accumulated depreciation. For a business, it is the same as equity, net worth, or shareholders' equity.

burden rate   The percentage rate at which a cost burden is added to particular other costs. The most common burden rates are the various overhead rates.

capital   The investment in a business, ordinarily equal to equity plus debt.

capital budgeting   The prediction of fixed asset investments that will be needed during the budget period.

capital expenditure   Purchase of buildings, equipment, tools, and the like, that will be accounted for as fixed assets and depreciated over a multiyear period.

cash   Currency, and monetary instruments that are equivalent to currency.

cash accounting   An accounting basis in which revenue, expense, and balance sheet items are recorded when cash is paid or received.

cash flow   The increase or decrease in the cash of a business over a particular period of time.

contribution margin   A percentage measure of profitability, equal to revenue minus variable or direct costs, divided by revenue. (The term is sometimes used for only the dollar amount of revenue minus variable or direct costs, although the latter is more often called contribution.)

cost   The amount of money spent to do or to buy something.

cost allocation   The process of assigning or charging one type of cost to other costs.

cost burden   The amount of cost added to a particular cost as the result of allocating another type of cost to it.

cost of goods sold   The direct costs of producing revenue, burdened by closely associated indirect costs. Also, beginning inventory plus purchases minus ending inventory. Often called cost of sales or cost of revenue.

cost pool   A grouping of costs for the purpose of allocation to, or identification with, particular cost centers, products, or services. Common cost pools are various overhead costs, general and administrative costs, and corporate costs.

current assets   Cash and those assets that will be converted into cash within a year.

current liabilities   Debts and payments that are due within a year.

current ratio   The ratio of current assets to current liabilities.

days inventory   The amount of inventory relative to the cost of goods sold, expressed in "days" typically as 365 times inventory divided by annual cost of goods sold.

days payables   The amount of payables relative to total material purchased, expressed in "days" typically as 365 times accounts payable divided by annual material purchases.

days receivables   The amount of accounts receivable relative to revenue, expressed in "days" typically as 365 times accounts receivable divided by annual revenue.

debt   Broadly, any liability. More narrowly and more commonly, money borrowed from, and owed to, another person or institution.

depreciation   The gradual decline in value of an asset because of use or age; the expense arising therefrom.

direct cost   Cost directly associated with production of specific revenue.

disbursement   An amount of cash paid out.

equity   The accounting value of a business, equal to assets minus liabilities. Commonly used interchangeably with book value, net asset value, net worth, and shareholders' equity.

expense   Past, current, or future cost that is charged to profit and loss during a period, in accordance with generally accepted accounting principles.

financial statement   An accounting document showing the financial status of a business or the results of business activity.

finished goods inventory   The portion of inventory that consists of goods and products ready for sale.

fiscal year   The twelve-month period for which financial results are prepared and reported. It may be different, by company choice, from the calendar year.

fixed assets   Assets whose life will extend beyond the

current accounting period: machinery, land, buildings, and the like.

fixed cost   A cost that does not vary with revenue over a relevant range of revenue amount.

fringe benefits   Payments by a company for things of value to, and for the use of, employees, such as insurance and vacations.

general and administrative expense *(G&A)*   Cost necessary to operate a business but not associated directly with the production of revenue, such as the cost of accounting.

Generally Accepted Accounting Principles (GAAP) The set of rules by and for the accounting profession that governs accounting practice and the preparation of financial statements.

gross margin   A measure of profitability, equal to revenue minus cost of goods sold divided by revenue. (The term is sometimes used for only the dollar amount of revenue minus cost of goods sold, although the latter is more often called gross profit.)

gross profit   *See* gross margin.

income statement   *See* profit and loss statement.

indirect cost   Cost not directly related or assignable to the production of specific revenue, products, or services.

inventory   The physical material and products that a business owns for future production of revenue.

liability   Something of value owed by a business. A valid claim that someone holds on assets of the business.

long-term debt   A debt that is not due for payment for more than one year.

long-term liability   An obligation that need not be discharged within one year.

margin   A percentage measure of profitability relative to revenue. (Also sometimes used as the dollar amount of revenue minus selected costs.) *See* contribution margin, gross margin, and profit margin.

markup   A measure of profitability equal to revenue minus cost (typically, direct cost or purchase cost) divided by that same cost. (The term is sometimes used for the dollar amount of revenue minus cost.)

net asset value   *See* equity.

net income   Revenue minus all expense for an accounting period, including federal and foreign income tax. In common usage, the same as profit after tax.

net worth   *See* equity.

operating statement   *See* profit and loss statement.

orders received   Binding agreements by customers to buy products or services from a company for future delivery.

overhead   Indirect cost. More often used to describe indirect cost in a particular function or activity, closely associated with production of revenue but not assignable to a particular product or service. Typical classes of overhead are manufacturing labor overhead, manufacturing material overhead, engineering overhead, and service overhead.

overhead pool   A cost pool for a particular type of overhead.

overhead rate   The percentage rate at which a particular overhead cost is added to particular direct cost, calculated by dividing the applicable overhead cost by the direct cost.

percentage of completion   A method of accounting, used for large and long contracts, that recognizes revenue during the course of the contract in accordance with the proportion of work that has been completed, or cost that has been incurred.

period cost   Cost expensed during the same period in which it is incurred.

prepaid expense   An asset representing an amount paid for purchases not yet received, i.e., a right to those purchases in the future.

prepaid revenue   A liability representing payment received for future products or services, i.e., an obligation to supply those products or services in the future.

present value   The equivalent value today of an amount of cash available in the future, with a specified interest rate.

profit   Revenue minus expense, the financial gain of a business.

profit and loss statement (P&L)   The financial statement that presents all revenue and expense and resulting profit or loss, by conventional categories, of a company for a time period. It is also called the income statement and the operating statement.

profit after tax   Revenue minus all expense, the same as net income.

profit before tax   Profit before accounting for federal and foreign income tax expense.

profit margin   A performance measure equal to revenue minus total expense divided by revenue.

raw materials inventory   The portion of inventory that consists of purchased material that will be used to make revenue-producing products, and the purchase cost of that material.

receipt   An amount of cash received.

return on assets   Profit divided by assets, a measure of the percentage of the value of its assets that is earned by the business.

return on capital   Profit divided by capital, a measure of the percentage of total investment earned by the business.

return on equity   Profit divided by equity, a measure of the percentage of the owners' investment earned by the business.

return on investment   For an entire business, synonymous with return on capital. For a given capital investment within a business, the ratio of the profit or cash flow that will result to the amount of the investment.

revenue   The amount of past, current, and future receipts that are earned and recorded in a given period, in accordance with Generally Accepted Accounting Principles.

sales Generally used interchangeably with revenue, but sometimes restricted to only the revenue that results from the purchase of products by customers (as opposed to, e.g., service revenue).

shareholders' equity Strictly speaking, the equity of a corporation, as opposed to a partnership or a proprietorship. Ordinarily used synonymously with equity, net worth, and net asset value.

short-term debt Debt that must be paid within a year.

short-term liability A liability that must be discharged within a year.

standard cost A calculated, anticipated cost of a product, used as expense when sale of that product is recorded on the P&L.

turnover The rate at which an asset is used and replaced, most often applied to inventory. It is expressed as the ratio of a year's revenue to the amount of the asset.

variable cost Cost that varies with revenue.

variance The amount by which an actual financial parameter, such as a cost, differs from its standard or budgeted value.

working capital Current assets minus current liabilities.

work in progress inventory The portion of inventory that consists of partially completed products, and the associated burdened labor and material costs.

NOTES

NOTES

NOTES

NOTES

NOTES

NOTES

NOTES

NOTES

NOTES

NOTES

NOTES